THE DISCIPLES OF JESUS

A Bible Study

Dean G. Blevins

THE FOUNDRY
PUBLISHING®

Copyright © 2023 by Dean G. Blevins

The Foundry Publishing®
PO Box 419527
Kansas City, MO 64141
thefoundrypublishing.com

ISBN 978-0-8341-4158-2

Printed in the
United States of America

Cover design: Caines Design
Interior design: Sharon Page

Library of Congress Cataloging-in-Publication Data
A complete catalog record for this book is available from the Library of Congress.

The internet addresses, email addresses, and phone numbers in this book are accurate at the time of publication. They are provided as a resource. The Foundry Publishing® does not endorse them or vouch for their content or permanence.

10 9 8 7 6 5 4 3 2 1

CONTENTS

⸺⟨∞⟩⸺

INTRODUCTION

❖ Before they were apostles, they were disciples, living alongside each other and in the presence of Jesus. Often people in churches come to know the disciples through a kind of larger-than-life vision of the men and women of Scripture. Christians often forget just how their own lives as disciples often mirror the day-to-day dispositions and reactions to life from long ago.

We need to remember that the disciples did not come to Jesus with some special set of qualifications. If they lived today, they would probably not have stellar résumés, wonderful social media profiles, or even seats in the front pew of the church. If we take a moment to contemplate the lives of the disciples, we find everyday people just like us coming to Jesus to be received and transformed by his presence. Often when we study the disciples, we begin by scrutinizing their humanity—perhaps even their fragility—if only to consider what they have in common with us. However, in and through the presence of Jesus, their everyday lives were transformed so that they became servants of the kingdom of God—and this is something that can happen to us as well.

What is more, the disciples also came *together.* Most writing, as well as preaching, tends to focus on each disciple as an individual. But do the disciples reveal more when considered in relationship to each other? Stopping long enough to consider the disciples in relationship, even in pairs, creates a different understanding and appreciation for what Jesus might have seen not only *within* each disciple but also *across* relationships.

This study looks at the disciples in their relationships with each other, mostly in pairs. Taking this side-by-side approach may provide a fresh appreciation of how we ourselves interact as disciples today. As the travelers discovered on the road to Emmaus (Luke 24:13-35), something radical can happen when Jesus appears in the middle of our relationships, during a journey, and when breaking bread together. Our study relies on both Scripture and early church tradition.[1] However, the accounts also include a bit of "scriptural imagination" that reflects the creativity of early church preaching. While there may be some biblical scholars who will wince at the material, my hope remains that the approach used here will make the disciples appear more accessible, more available, to our lives today.

---

1. Information from Christian tradition adapted primarily from the following sources: Paul J. Achtemeier, ed., *The HarperCollins Bible Dictionary,* rev. ed. (New York: HarperCollins, 1996); F. L. Cross and E. A. Livingstone, eds., *The Oxford Dictionary of the Christian Church,* 3rd ed. (New York: Oxford University Press, 1997).

one

ACTION HEROES
Simon Peter and Andrew

❖ Our journey begins with two of the best-known disciples, Simon Peter and his brother Andrew. Sibling relationships shape the four most prominent disciples: Peter with Andrew, and James with John. All four disciples appear early in the Synoptic Gospels: Matthew 4:18-22; Mark 1:16-20; and Luke 5:1-11.[1] Andrew and Peter also appear early in John's Gospel (1:35-42).[2] Three disciples—Peter, John, and James—form what might be called Jesus's inner circle, with Andrew as a close associate.

---

1. M. Eugene Boring, "The Synoptic Problem," in *HarperCollins Bible Dictionary*, 1082. "Synoptic" means "as one view," which describes how the first three gospels tend to mirror each other in many accounts, though not always arranged in the same manner.

2. Laura S. Holmes and George Lyons, *John 1–12*, New Beacon Bible Commentary (Kansas City: Beacon Hill Press of Kansas City, 2020), 34-40.

Simon Peter

Outside the life and work of the apostle Paul, perhaps no disciple gains as much attention in the New Testament as Simon, son of Jonah, whom Jesus would call Peter (John 1:42). This is especially so in the Gospels, and in fact, many believe the gospel writer Mark was a close friend of Peter.[3] Where does one begin to understand who Peter was and what he offered as a person?

I love the story of Peter *after* the resurrection of Jesus. Peter, in John 21, decides to go fishing (v. 3). After a fruitless night, Jesus appears and provides the kind of advice you might hear from an old-time fisherman, with dramatic results. When the disciple John recognizes Jesus, he shouts, "It is the Lord!" (v. 7). Peter then puts on his clothes and jumps into the sea, leaving the other disciples to do the work of hauling their catch of fish to shore. The scene is actually kind of humorous. Just imagine Peter wrestling on his outer garment as he walks off the edge of the boat while the rest of the disciples plead for help. You could almost see Peter wading out of the water to the shoreline, dripping from head to toe.

This view of the "all wet" Peter really reminds us of the disciple's impulsiveness. Peter always seems to be the one person who lives by the motto "Leap before you look." Peter was the one who tried to follow Jesus by stepping out onto the stormy waves of Galilee but then needed Jesus to rescue

---

3. Kent Brower, *Mark*, New Beacon Bible Commentary (Kansas City: Beacon Hill Press of Kansas City, 2012), 26-31.

him (Matt. 14:28-30). One can find Peter accompanying John into Jerusalem to help prepare the upper room for the Last Supper (Luke 22:8), but Peter also falls asleep during Jesus's anguished prayer in the garden of Gethsemane (Matt. 26:40-46). Later Peter is the one who strikes out in anger at temple guards during Jesus's arrest (John 18:10-11).

Along with all these actions, Peter, perhaps most significantly, was also among those who immediately "stepped out" and left everything when he heard Jesus's invitation to follow him (Luke 5:11). Peter's first inclination was always to move—to step out. Maybe that is why Jesus acknowledged that walking would characterize the end of Peter's life, even though it would mean being led by others to a place he least wanted to go (John 21:18-19). Most poignantly, though, among Jesus's final words to Peter is the same invitation that Peter heard when he began his walk with the Lord: "Follow me" (v. 19).

When he wasn't moving his body, Peter was moving his lips. Peter's second motto seems to have been, "Speak first and listen later." However, Peter's words sometimes reveal a man willing to confess his limitations and sinfulness before the lordship of Jesus (Luke 5:8). This is surprising when we consider that Peter was probably one of the more self-sufficient disciples. Not only was he married (Matt. 8:14; Mark 1:29-34; Luke 4:38-39), but he also could maintain (by the standards of the time) a household. Yet he remained aware not only of his sinfulness but also his calling to join Jesus, whom he later confessed to be "the Messiah, the Son of the living God" (Matt. 16:16-19).

Peter's confession of Jesus's messiahship and sonship serves as the rock[4] on which Peter would stand alongside the rest of the church. Yet Peter, soon after this confession, rebukes Jesus for predicting his impending death and receives Jesus's rebuke in return: "Get behind me, Satan!" (v. 23). Even Peter's response to Jesus's encounter with Moses and Elijah on the Mount of Transfiguration was subject to rebuke (17:1-13). Peter, taken up in the moment, proposes to turn a transforming vision into a shrine honoring all three leaders. God the Father intervenes to instruct Peter concerning Jesus, who is truly the Lord, the true Son of God (v. 5). Although Peter was quick to confess Jesus as the Anointed One, his understanding of that confession took much longer to develop.

Not only did Peter misunderstand Jesus as Lord, but he especially misunderstood Jesus as Suffering Servant. When confronted by Jesus's desire to wash Peter's feet, Peter at first resists but then goes too far and asks to be washed from toe to head, for which he again is gently reproved (John 13:3-11). Later that same night, Jesus foretells his own death and Peter attempts to block the way by asserting that he will sacrifice his own life for Jesus's. Unfortunately, this declaration receives in return Jesus's painful pronouncement that Peter will betray him three times (vv. 36-38). Jesus's pronouncement becomes all too true as Peter later does indeed finally deny his Lord and

---

4. Scholars disagree about whether Peter the man or Peter's confession of Jesus as Messiah provides that rock or foundation. In this book we will give consideration to both possibilities. Both Peter and his confession can be conceived as rocks and as foundational for the church.

suffering Savior three times (Matt. 26:69-75; Mark 14:66-72; Luke 22:54-62; John 18:25-27).

———∞∞∞———

When confident, and even when in doubt, Simon Peter would *do* something.

———∞∞∞———

It is not surprising that Jesus, following his resurrection, lovingly confronts Peter in John 21 with a clear question, asked three times: "Simon son of John, do you love me?" (vv. 15-17). Much is made of Jesus's admonitions (feeding and tending sheep and lambs) following Peter's responses, but the repetition of the question probably assured, in contrast to the earlier denials, that Peter's first word would indeed be his final word. Jesus guides Peter, a man who would speak first and then sometimes do an about-face, to painfully think through his heartfelt love for the Savior.

We may think this view of Peter is very unflattering. What could Jesus see in this impulsive disciple? What is it about Peter that caused our Savior to call Peter the rock, the foundation, on which the church would be built?[5] Perhaps Simon Peter's actions provide a clue. Understanding Peter includes acknowledging his bias toward action. When confident, and even when in doubt, Simon Peter would *do* something. If impulse implies a commitment to act, Peter seemed more than willing to act out his faith and follow Jesus. Peter stepped out onto water, into fights, and into following Jesus regardless of the circumstances. Faith for Peter could not be separated from action, from conduct, from even proclamation (Acts 4:8-12; 5:27-30). Peter did not see faith as a private possession but as a commission, a response to the core invitation to follow Jesus and live a life of discipleship every moment of every day.

Peter also acted and spoke as he thought. Rather than taking the time for reflection, Peter verbalized his thoughts, making them transparent before Jesus. This approach brought both moments of deep insight ("You are the Messiah") and provided moments of deep insecurity ("You cannot be crucified"; "I do not know this Jesus"; "What about John?").[6] Peter's trust of Jesus allowed for Peter's transparency before Jesus. Perhaps Peter's ability not only to speak freely but also to receive admonition undergirded his first address to skeptics and believers in Acts 2. Who else would have had the inclination, if not the Spirit-filled ability among the disciples, to immediately take up the challenge?

5. Ibid.
6. Author paraphrases.

Andrew

But what about Andrew? If Peter portrays an active faith, reflected in his own agency if not his ability, how might Peter's brother fit into this journey? Perhaps the most telling story of Andrew starts at the beginning, since he is often known as the *Prōtoklētos* (Greek for "first called").[7] The Gospel of John tells us the most about Andrew. From John 1:35-42, we know that he was first a disciple of John the Baptist and that he brought Peter to Jesus with the proclamation, "We have found the Messiah" (v. 41). Later, rather than complaining about Jesus's admonition to the disciples to help him feed five thousand people, Andrew brings a young boy with five loaves and two fish, which Jesus turns into a miraculous feast (6:8-9). Finally, Andrew served, along with Philip, as a go-between to inform Jesus that a group of Greeks wished to see him (12:20-22).

Like Peter, Andrew also seems to possess a kind of bias toward action, but more as a catalyst. Rather than being out in front like his brother, Andrew displays a strategic ability to see a need and fill it. When we look at Jesus's journey with the disciples, we begin to see Andrew as an organizer, a quarter-master, a relational networker. Andrew channeled his impulses into other people, encouraging, enabling, and resourcing others to inspire them to action. Ori Brafman and Rod A. Beckstrom, in their book *The Starfish and the Spider*, note that almost all movements require two leaders, often in tandem.

---

7. W. Brian Shelton, *Quest for the Historical Apostles: Tracing Their Lives and Legacies* (Grand Rapids: Baker, 2018), 96.

One they describe as the "hero," out in front, providing a vision, compelling people to respond. The other they call the "catalyst," often working behind the scenes to provide opportunity, direction, and resources as people join the movement.[8] Simon Peter's natural impulsive action reflects his ability, through Jesus's instruction and the power of the Holy Spirit, to become the first "heroic" apostle of the church. Andrew possesses the catalytic ability to complement this effort both among the disciples and later as a leader living out his own active ministry.

Andrew channeled his impulses into other people, encouraging, enabling, and resourcing others to inspire them to action.

---

8. Ori Brafman and Rod A. Beckstrom, *The Starfish and the Spider: The Unstoppable Power of Leaderless Organizations* (New York: Portfolio, 2006), 85-131.

Joining the Journey

Ultimately the brothers Peter and Andrew do remind us that discipleship demands action. Their desire to live out their faith in following Jesus served them in their missional efforts later in life. Peter proved willing to stand before the Sanhedrin, with the apostle John, in Acts. Peter's actions also led to his imprisonment for his faith by Herod (Acts 12:3-19). Peter also journeyed to Caesarea to meet with Cornelius and then returned to Jerusalem with a mandate to reach out to the Gentiles (Acts 10). Apparently even Peter's wife journeyed with him on future missionary efforts (1 Cor. 9:5). According to Christian tradition, Peter traveled to Rome and (as Jesus noted in John 21) was crucified, upside down.[9]

We all need to be ready and willing to live out our faith as disciples. You might look at this willingness as an embrace of our calling or vocation before Jesus Christ. Living out this faith may come with fits and starts, as it did with Peter. Those fits and starts often occur when we encounter people in our everyday lives, as well as unexpected successes and challenges. At times, we may feel more comfortable being like Andrew, willing to serve as a facilitator, networker, and resource provider for the church. Yet even Andrew risked telling his brother of the promise of Jesus Christ when the opportunity presented itself, and together, they both left John the Baptist to follow Jesus. For Andrew, that journey, as Christian tradi-

---

9. *Oxford Dictionary of the Christian Church*, 3rd ed. (1997), s.v. "Peter, St."

tion tells us, meant traveling to southern Greece, where he was later crucified on an X-shaped cross.[10]

Perhaps when emphasizing discipleship, the church focuses too much on times of reflection and withdrawal. For many people, discipleship remains an active endeavor. Regardless, discipleship is not a spectator sport. We all must be willing to live out our faith and obedience with Jesus. If anything, the brothers Peter and Andrew remind us that the command to follow requires deliberate action. We might not always know where Jesus will lead us, but we must be willing to take to the road and begin walking.

---

10. *Oxford Dictionary of the Christian Church*, 3rd ed. (1997), s.v. "Andrew, St."

Discussion Questions

1. Can you name certain times when people might "leap before they look"? What motivates people to act first and then explain their actions later? When might acting this way be necessary?

2. Some people are known as "verbal processors"—that is, they think out loud by talking to people. How might this approach create problems or provide opportunities?

3. Looking over the life of Simon Peter, why do you think he demonstrated such wide swings between absolute support and complete betrayal?

4. This chapter identifies Andrew as a catalyst or a facilitator-networker. Why are such people important for churches or communities?

5. Are there aspects of Peter's or Andrew's life that you see in yourself? How might their lives in the presence of Jesus help you to understand your discipleship?

Scripture Studies: Will the Real Peter Stand Up? Positive and Negative Portrayals of Peter

- Walking on Water: Matthew 14:22-33
- Proclamation of Jesus and "Get Behind Me, Satan": Matthew 16:13-27
- Taking a Bath: John 13:3-10
- Confessing and Denying Jesus: John 13:36-38; Luke 22:54-62
- Love Me, Love Me Not: John 21:15-17

two

LOVING SONS OF THUNDER
James and John

❖ If the brothers Andrew and Peter are examples of action, the brothers James and John seem to provide a contrast in temperament. The brothers together were known as the "Boanerges," or "sons of thunder" (Mark 3:17, NIV). Their reputation seems well deserved when, in Samaria, James and John wanted to call down fire from heaven on a village for its lack of hospitality (see Luke 9:52-55). What might have prompted such a "fiery" disposition?

James and John

We do know that the two brothers were the sons of Zebedee and partners to Peter. Perhaps their social status provides the first clue to their nature. While Peter and Andrew seem somewhat independent, James and John still worked for their father's fishing enterprise. Admittedly, this difference in social status is awfully tenuous, since all the Galilean disciples lived closer to the subsistence level. However, these two young men probably found it personally irritating to continue to work and live, whether because of economic dependence or age, under the shadow of their father.

Perhaps, much like Peter, the true nature of the brothers appears later in the Gospels. There seems to be no doubt that James and John were part of Jesus's inner circle. The two men, along with Peter, were present at the Mount of Transfiguration, where Jesus meets both Moses and Elijah, in brilliance, and when Peter speaks (probably first) and is reprimanded by God the Father (Matt. 17:1-9; Mark 9:2-10; Luke 9:28-36). Following this event, Jesus predicts his death one more time (Matt. 17:22-23; Mark 9:30-32; Luke 9:43-45). Whereas Peter denies Jesus's commitment to suffer and die, the brothers take a different approach and ask to sit at Jesus's right and left hand (Mark 10:35-45). The request is also placed on the lips of the boys' mother in Matthew 20:20-23. As someone who grew up in the southeastern part of the United States, I am not sure which could be worse: having the impertinence to request this special status, an assumed privilege, on their own or to stand silent and be considered "mama's boys" by letting their mother make this request. Jesus responded that James and John would share the "cup" of Jesus's suffering but that the positions they sought were not for Jesus to bestow (Mark 10:38-40). James, in Acts 12:1-5, later experienced this "cup" while fulfilling God's will.[1]

---

1. Shelton, *Quest for the Historical Apostles*, 117.

The rest of the disciples, in both the Gospels of Mark and Matthew, react with anger when they hear about the brothers' request for special honor, sparking a massive debate about who indeed is the greatest among the disciples. Apparently, these fiery young men are capable of sparking an intensive disagreement among the faithful. Jesus reminds the disciples that to be great they must possess a servant's heart (Matt. 20:20-28; Mark 10:35-45). This is akin to what Jesus also said when he equated greatness in the kingdom of heaven to having a childlike faith (Matt. 18:1-5).

Peter and James are the logical right-hand and even left-hand men to Jesus.

Why would the brothers James and John seek such status? Why attempt to leave behind Peter, the other member of Jesus's inner circle? If we take a moment to speculate on their motives, we may discover something about the humanity of both brothers. If Mark's list of the twelve disciples includes an implicit ranking of the disciples, then Peter is named before James and John (3:13-19). Matthew's account (10:2-4) and

Luke's list (6:12-16) even include Andrew before the two sons of Zebedee. While both brothers remain in the inner circle, Peter is the most recognized leader, with Jesus pronouncing Peter as "the rock" and the foundation of the church. Perhaps the two brothers' request to sit at the right and left of Jesus was an attempt to secure recognition for their leadership alongside Peter. The move may have been particularly important for John, the youngest brother and perhaps the youngest of the disciples. Even Mark goes further to stress James as the son of Zebedee, followed by John, the brother of James (3:17). Mark's more exclusive listing seems to show that Peter and James are the logical right-hand and even left-hand men to Jesus.

With Jesus predicting his departure, would James and John really go so far as to request Jesus to secure their status? After all, some scholars suggest that the brothers may very well have been related to Jesus through their mother, Salome, the sister of Mary the mother of Christ (Matt. 27:56; Mark 16:1). We also know that Andrew and Simon Peter first followed John the Baptist, a relative to Christ, with Mary being a cousin of John the Baptist's mother, Elizabeth (Luke 1:39-56). Who really represented the people truly closest to Jesus? John provides a clue.

John and James

Perhaps it is not surprising that John, the younger brother, and perhaps youngest disciple, found himself beloved by Jesus, and this identity sufficed for defining who he was. John's Gospel does not insist that the anonymous "disciple whom Jesus loved" (John 13:21-30; 19:26-27; 21:7; etc.) is both John and the Gospel's writer. Some biblical scholars question whether they are the same. However, most biblical scholars concede that the writer and the anonymous recipient of Jesus's love is the one and the same John.[2]

Love places John at the foot of the cross, where Jesus charges this young disciple with the responsibility of caring for Mary, Jesus's mother.

The Gospel of John also reveals one of the most intimate portrayals of Jesus in the upper room (chs. 14–17). Jesus's gathering with the disciples in the upper room in Jerusalem occurs in all four gospels (Matt. 26:17-30; Mark 14:12-26; Luke 22:7-38; and John 13:1-35). Yet John, reclining next to Jesus at the table in the upper room (John 13:23), takes the time to record

---

2. Holmes and Lyons, *John 1–12*, 38-40.

some of the most intimate moments of Jesus with his disciples. Later, even as other disciples were in hiding following Jesus's arrest, love places John at the foot of the cross, where Jesus charges this young disciple with the responsibility of caring for Mary, Jesus's mother (19:26-27). This remarkable commission of love occurs even as John's own mother stands at the same cross (Matt. 27:56). Finally, love calls John on the shoreline to join Jesus and Peter, where now his reputation for faithfulness and his love for telling Jesus's story provide the finishing narrative (John 21:20-25).

It may seem odd that the younger John would be more well known than even his brother James. Still, it seems fair to say that the love for Jesus eventually displaced the anxious desire for recognition. Some people do need greater recognition and opportunities to lead in the church. However, under Jesus's tutelage, both brothers in time set aside their anxiety for recognition while also accepting the mantle of leadership. Some rivalry may have remained between Peter and John, at least as far as John beating Peter in a footrace (John 20:3-4), but John also gave deference to Peter, allowing him to enter the empty tomb first (vv. 5-10). The two men may have entered the tomb separately, but they returned together, walking side by side.

Later, in the book of Acts, both James and John proved to be leaders in the church right alongside Peter, as even the apostle Paul testifies in Galatians 2:9. James finally did drink from the painful cup from which Jesus drank (Matt. 20:22; Mark 10:28). As the leader of the church in Jerusalem, James was executed (probably beheaded) on orders from Herod Agrippa I. This account sets James apart not only in his leadership but also as the only one of the twelve disciples whose martyrdom was reported in Scripture (Acts 12:2).[3]

John and Peter would stand together, side by side, teaching and even defending their mission of proclaiming the gospel to Jewish leaders (4:1-22) and later reaching again into Samaria (8:14-25). Whatever acrimony created in the original request for status alongside Jesus now lay in the past. Love, solidarity, leadership, and mission were what the brothers stood for alongside Peter. That solidarity may have propelled John later through Asia Minor and ultimately to Ephesus.[4]

Joining the Journey

It might prove charitable to recognize that both sons of Zebedee exhibited leadership. They lived inside Jesus's closest circle. Yet when facing the strange mix of family heritage and social station, perhaps both men, particularly John, feared they would not be recognized for the leaders they could become.

In our day, we often discover that the ability to lead and the opportunity to demonstrate leadership do not always go hand in hand. Often insecurity arises early when we wrestle with our place in discipleship. Sometimes, due to our own her-

---

3. *Oxford Dictionary of the Christian Church*, 3rd ed. (1997), s.v. "James, St., 'the Great.'"

4. *Oxford Dictionary of the Christian Church*, 3rd ed. (1997), s.v. "John, St."

itage, the color of our skin, our gender, our social status, we, too, wrestle with recognition, opportunity, and, yes, enough status to exercise the qualities of leadership we might rise to if given the chance. Fear of being overlooked, left out, or left behind in learning to exercise our leadership gifts might push us toward the same need as the two brothers.

People might even feel challenged based on their allegiances. This appears to be the case when the "sons of thunder" took exception and tried to hinder the efforts of another person casting out demons in Jesus's name (Mark 9:38-40). The brothers might have wondered, "How dare this person even pretend to be part of the faithful!" Yet Jesus cautioned the brothers that allegiance and action did not always come with relational privilege. So what might free these two brothers from the fear of being left out, losing status, and losing leadership?

Love

How did Jesus select his inner circle? Did he choose the group members on the basis of their innate leadership? Or were they just the first to join and Jesus had a limited "founders" group? Did Jesus hope to "influence the influencers" through the group? If so, Peter's impulsiveness and James and John's ability to sow dissension among the disciples made all three poor influencers. Instead, perhaps all three disciples needed Jesus's loving presence in their lives amid their all-too-human limitations. James and John struggled to live into the kind of leadership they would later demonstrate as leaders in the book of Acts. They needed Jesus's continued love to both mute their lightning-like dispositions and alleviate their apprehension about whether or not they truly deserved to lead. To become the leaders Christ intended them to be, the brothers needed Jesus's caring mentorship and careful advocacy.

The same may be so in our day. We all may be capable of leadership, but releasing insecurities, together with accepting guidance, takes time and grace.

Discussion Questions

1. Why would some people feel insecure about their lives? What might cause them to be hot tempered at the same time?

2. How might love help someone who is insecure?

3. Why would James and John's request to sit as Jesus's right and left hand put them at odds with Peter?

4. How can a common purpose overcome a "friendly" rivalry between people?

5. How might acknowledging Jesus's love and calling in our lives overcome any sense of insecurity or alleviate irritation caused by rivalries?

Scripture Studies: Will the Real James and John Stand Up? Positive and Negative Portrayals of James and John

- Fiery Dispositions: Mark 9:38-40; Luke 9:52-55
- Who Made the Request? Mark 10:35-45; Matthew 20:20-28
- A Race to the Finish Line: John 20:3-4; 21:20-25
- Standing Up for Jesus: Acts 4:1-22; 8:14-25

three

BORDER CROSSERS
Matthew and Philip

❖ So far the pairing of the disciples has been with family members. Whether comparing Andrew with Peter, or James with John, the similarities of behavior are clearly depicted in Scripture. As we proceed, the challenge to determine what disciples have in common will be more difficult. Scripture does not always offer sufficient information, just snippets of detail that emerge from the Gospels. Christian tradition (writings such as *Ecclesiastical History*, written by early Christian historian Eusebius) provides additional information, but that material reflects a different approach.[1]

Histories around the disciples and/or apostles really reflect stories that we often tell of our family members, rather than journalistic accounts. While growing up, I often heard stories about family members from the past. Some were ac-

---

1. Shelton, *Quest for the Historical Apostles*, 1-4.

counts of heroic actions; others were cautionary tales. While often larger than life, the stories possessed a kernel of truth usually buried in the love and humor of the storyteller. By contrast, during a stint as a journalist, I wrestled to get the basic facts and present the best account of a particular event. However, I realized that I could never get to the "right" truth, since the very people we often interviewed and the information we collected remained imperfect. Yet we sought to do the best reporting of the information we possessed, as fairly and impartially as possible, in a straightforward way.

Christian tradition often lies somewhere between these two different types of narration. The tradition hopes to be fair but often remains committed to the larger-than-life tales about the disciples, now apostles. So the recounting will both honor and somewhat embellish the kernels of information if only to inspire other members of the Christian family. An example comes from the two brothers of the previous chapter. The absence of James in John's Gospel (possibly because he was the brother who spoke to Jesus about calling down fire on a village or about bestowing privileges to the brothers) raises questions for journalists. Later stories of James as the founder of the Christian faith in Spain seem more like family tales, particularly when Christians discover a grave site for James's body in the ninth century that serves to inspire pilgrimages and encourage resistance against Moorish invaders.[2] The "leg-

---

2. Asbury Smith, *The Twelve Christ Chose* (New York: Harper Brothers, 1958), 41-48.

end" of Saint James weaves multiple stories. And so do other stories about Matthew and Philip.

Matthew

Thinking of Matthew as a larger-than-life person may appear difficult when we consider the disciple's profession. Matthew was a tax collector, one of the more despised professions in the land of Jerusalem. If James could inspire an entire country, Matthew would be the kind of person most people would rather forget. But just naming the disciple generates the kind of journalistic questions that we often face. Biblical scholars, thinking like journalists, often wrestle with the question of whether Matthew, the tax collector, in Matthew 9:9 (often associated with the author of the Gospel of Matthew) is also the tax collector Levi in Mark 2:14 and Luke 5:27. If Simon received the new name Peter (or *Petros*, which is Greek for "rock") from Jesus, could Matthew merely be the same person with a new name and later listed as the eighth disciple in Matthew 10:2-4? Some scholars think so. However, other scholars argue that Levi is also known as the son of Alphaeus in Mark 2:14. Later, in the different lists of the disciples (see Mark 3:14-19; Luke 6:14-16; as well as Matt. 10:2-4), James the Lesser is introduced as the son of Alphaeus; however, there is no indication that Matthew, as Levi, and James are brothers. Also, both Levi and Matthew remain Semitic names—that is, they are not changed to Greek names (which may prove important later). Finally, the Gospel of Luke introduces a third tax collector, Zacchaeus, who follows Jesus as he passes through Jericho (Luke 19:1-10). Whether or not Matthew is one disciple among two or three tax collectors, perhaps he might say, "Well, misery loves company."

As noted, tax collectors occupied one of the lower rungs of the most despised social classes. Tax collectors often served as customs agents or, worse, bagmen for a numbers racket or loan shark. Tax collectors often levied tax fees up to 30 or 40 percent more than expected. Unfortunately, the taxpayers also knew that the Roman government, much like gangsters, never paid off. Money was taken, but little service was rendered for Jewish people or their Gentile counterparts in outpost regions such as Galilee or Judah. Matthew dealt with the lowest of the low, was seen as a traitor to his Jewish roots, and remained minuscule by Jewish social standards.

Philip

We seem to know even less about Philip, our second disciple, than the muddied history of Matthew. John's Gospel notes that Philip comes from Bethsaida, the same city as Andrew and Peter, near the northern point of the Sea of Galilee (John 1:44). Philip also introduced Nathanael to Jesus (whom we will encounter in the next chapter) and seemed to know enough Old Testament Scriptures to back up that invitation (vv. 45-46). Jesus questioned Philip about how to feed the five thousand (6:1-8), and Philip's frank answer that six months' wages would not do the job reveals his practical mind (as contrasted with Andrew's putting forward the boy with five loaves and two fishes in vv. 8-9). This same practical mind probably sparked Philip's request that Jesus reveal God the Father during the Upper Room Discourse (14:8-9).

However, we can find another account of Philip that might reveal his importance as a disciple alongside that of Matthew. John 12:20-26 begins an interesting story in which Greeks approach Philip for an audience with Jesus. Philip and Andrew communicate this request to Jesus. Jesus's response might surprise readers. Jesus sees this request by Greeks, or Gentiles, as a signal of his impending glorification through death and resurrection. The passage ends with a clear call to discipleship—that is, a call to leave behind the cares of this world in order to follow and serve Jesus. Why would Philip serve a pivotal role in this story?

What Philip embodied in his name and person reflected the kind of cultural and ethnic diversity that signaled to Jesus that the kingdom of God was coming for all people.

Philip, we know, possessed a Greek name (meaning, "he who loves horses"), which, apparently, he carried from birth. Philip may well have been a "God-fearer," or a non-Jewish sympathizer to Judaism. Jesus would rename Simon, whose family name designated him as the "son of Jonah" (Matt. 16:17) or "son of John" (John 21:15-17) and who demonstrated a clear Jewish lineage. Simon's new name, the Greek name Peter, might reveal the Son of God's intention to reach out to both Jew and Gentile. However, Philip already possessed a Greek name and probably connections within the Greek community. So Philip, not Peter, held a natural affinity with Greeks for them to approach him and gain access to Jesus. Philip, in his very personhood, could cross the boundaries between Greeks and Jews. Just as Andrew facilitated the meeting between his brother Simon and Jesus, so also did Andrew know that he could facilitate through Philip a meeting between the Greeks and Jesus.

What Philip embodied in his name and person reflected the kind of cultural and ethnic diversity that signaled to Jesus that the kingdom of God was coming for all people. Philip would not be the last important "Greek" representative for the early church. Acts 6:1-7 recounts an intercultural conflict between the Hellenists and Hebrews (Greeks and Jews) over the care of widows. To resolve the issue, the apostles ask the church to select seven men, whom they then appoint as deacons to minister in their stead. All the selected men (including Stephen, who would later stand out for his speech and subsequent martyrdom [Acts 7]) have Greek names and thus no doubt a Greek heritage. We might imagine Philip standing with the other apostles as he sees Jesus's vision now being lived out in church leadership.

Perhaps Matthew also stands out as a person able to cross boundaries, in this case with those who were viewed as society's most repulsive members. Matthew responded to Jesus's invitation by serving as a host to a most unusual banquet (Matt. 9:10-13). Alongside the disciples, we find Matthew's table surrounded by other "tax collectors and sinners" (v. 10). One might wonder who was worse—the sinners who did not follow Jewish customs or the tax collectors, often considered the most ungodly people one could meet.

Matthew filled the table with people he probably knew best, those on the very margins of society. While not perhaps as socially connected or sophisticated as a chief tax collector like Zacchaeus (whose name, amazingly, means "innocent" or "pure"), Matthew probably knew and taxed people both within and beyond the Jewish faith. Culture, much less social status, tends to get lost by those living on the margins of social respectability. Matthew's friends may well have come from those margins of society. Yet Jesus declares that he lives to call those selfsame people to repentance, to healing, to merciful love (Matt. 9:12-13; Mark 2:13-17; Luke 5:27-32). Only someone like Matthew, because of his social status, could cross the boundaries and bring these people to the party.

Christian tradition continues the stories of Philip and Matthew. Many might assume that the disciple Philip also evangelized the Ethiopian eunuch on the road to Gaza (Acts

8:26-40) and continued onward, preaching in towns along his journey to Caesarea. However, this was the *deacon* Philip, who was listed alongside Stephen with the other Greek-speaking deacons of Acts 6. Philip the disciple, now apostle, continued to cross boundaries by later living and preaching in Scythia, or what is known as Ukraine today. Other accounts state that Philip died by being crucified on a tall cross at Hierapolis of Phrygia, or modern-day Turkey. That story may be why some Christian traditions symbolize Philip with a tall cross as well as the loaves and fishes associated with the feeding of the five thousand.[3]

If we listen to the same family stories from Christian tradition about Matthew, we will hear that he ministered to a number of global regions: Persia, Macedonia, Syria, Parthia, Media and, perhaps doing one better than the deacon Philip, Ethiopia. Stories from Christian tradition also suggest that Matthew died a martyr. The Christian symbol for Matthew is sometimes a bag of coins in reference to his occupation as a tax collector.[4]

Joining the Journey

Hearing the story of Matthew reminds us that Jesus demonstrates both the desire and power to reach people on the margins of society. No matter how questionable our back-

---

3. *Oxford Dictionary of the Christian Church*, 3rd ed. (1997), s.v. "Philips in the New Testament."

4. *Oxford Dictionary of the Christian Church*, 3rd ed. (1997), s.v. "Matthew, St."

ground, no matter how broken our previous actions might be, Jesus invites us to the table to break bread and dine with him. No one lives beyond the saving grace of God. For those of us more fortunate, we need to keep in mind that Jesus does not check a person's pedigree before admitting her or him to the church. We need to provide the hospitality worthy of the body of Christ.

The story of Matthew reminds us that Jesus demonstrates both the desire and power to reach people on the margins of society. No matter how questionable our background, no matter how broken our previous actions might be, Jesus invites us to the table to break bread and dine with him.

Philip reminds us that the ability to cross boundaries to reach those in other cultures remains a major challenge. Having people who know not only the language but also the customs and diverse cultures of other communities serves as a key asset for the gospel. Jesus's vision of a kingdom that invites all people, all cultures, remains at the core of the gospel message. Unfortunately, when one culture gains ascendance over others—such as Judaism in first-century Palestine or Western culture in much of the world today—people tend to conflate that culture with the gospel or even the kingdom of God. However, Philip the disciple reminds us (as do later Stephen and the deacon Philip) that, at times, believers need to work less at Christianizing a different culture and more at recognizing how embedded their own version of Christianity is with their culture. This recognition opens the way for the church not only to listen to those able to cross cultural boundaries but also to correct the embedded assumptions of the dominant culture. Jesus gave Simon Peter a Greek name to help him reach out to Gentiles, a task he would succeed at in Acts 10 but would later fail in Galatians 2:12-13. Philip possessed within himself a kind of cultural awareness that could empower Greeks to find Jesus.

What connects these two disciples, either by name or by social station, may be their ability to cross boundaries. Before they did so as apostles, they lived in boundary-crossing worlds. Be it cultural differences or social marginalization, they could speak to people and hospitably invite them to meet

Jesus. That ability demonstrates a gift that we need to understand and appreciate in our day.

Discussion Questions

1. Can you name some people who we might consider to
   be living on the margins of society?

2. Why might cross-cultural ministry present a signifi-
   cant challenge?

3. Why would Jesus seek to reach out to and through several tax collectors?

4. Can you name either a person or a group who many
   people would be surprised to see in the church but
   who would make an excellent witness for Jesus?

5. Who might Jesus call you to welcome and embrace as
   a disciple?

Scripture Studies: Ministry from the Margins of Jewish Tradition

- Lessons from the Margins: John 12:20-22; Matthew 9:9-13
- Tax Collectors' Invitation: Luke 5:27-32; 19:1-10
- Two Greek Servants: Acts 6:1-8; 8:4-8, 26-40

four

BORN SKEPTICS
Nathanael and Thomas

❖ If our last two disciples, Philip and Matthew, seem to connect and relate more with Andrew and Peter, perhaps our next
two disciples reflect more the dispositions of James and John.
If James and John embodied the metaphor of a violent thun-
derstorm, Nathanael and Thomas seem to personify a gloomy
morning that makes a person want to go back to bed. Nathanael
and Thomas could dampen the spirits of just about anyone.

Nathanael

Nathanael is also known as Bartholomew, which in Aramaic means the "son of Talmai" (Mark 3:18; Matt. 10:3). The
story of Nathanael's calling begins in John 1:43-49. In verse
43, Philip, the boundary crosser from our last chapter, receives
a direct invitation from Jesus to follow him. Philip then finds
Nathanael and exclaims, "We have found him about whom
Moses in the Law and also the Prophets wrote, Jesus son of
Joseph from Nazareth" (John 1:45). We can almost hear the

excitement in Philip's voice about this discovery. Nathanael replies, "Can anything good come out of Nazareth?" (v. 46). Nathanael's simple reply signals a posture that feels pretty familiar today. We know Nathanael's home is Cana of Galilee (21:2), where Jesus would turn water into wine during a wedding (2:1-12). The exact location of Cana, however, remains a contested subject, though many Bible maps place the town in the northern section of Galilee rather than the southern sector, where Nazareth was located. Could Nathanael's question reflect some village rivalry between Nazareth and Cana?

Nathanael, the skeptic, represents the kind of people who love to raise questions to an artform.

Nathanael was likely questioning how one so exalted could come from such a lowly, rural township like Nazareth (a recurring theme that Jesus faced in John 18:5-7; 19:19; Acts 6:14; 24:5). Even Matthew, writing his gospel, takes time to defend Jesus's Nazarene lineage during his account of Jesus's childhood (Matt. 2:19-23). Nathanael's incredulous response probably reflects the popular expectations of who the Messiah might be and where the Messiah might reside. Yet the hyperbole "Can *anything* good come from Nazareth?" reflects a deeper skepticism than other responses might entail. Why?

Possibly Nathanael, the skeptic, represents the kind of people who love to raise questions to an artform by questioning the very sanity of the person delivering the news—namely, Philip. Skepticism, particularly skeptical questions, really touches a nerve in most people.

This brings to mind the two words young children possess that inevitably drive parents crazy. The first word is "no." And the second word is "why." When a young child begins the game of "why," even the mildest-mannered, well-educated adult can be reduced to emotional distress. Each adult answer often invites the child's repeated question *why*. If any adult can answer five consecutive "whys" without resorting to the response "Go ask your mother [or father or teacher or the neighbor next door or *anyone* else]," she or he has earned the parenting merit badge for the day. The repeated questioning often picks us apart, pushing our assumptions and slowly deconstructing our self-assuredness. Repeated questioning causes us to seek solace anywhere we can find it.

Children normally open this line of questioning out of sheer curiosity. Skeptics learn how to threaten others by just beginning the conversation with a challenge buried in the question. Even offering an answer undoubtedly opens a new line of questioning, a fresh challenge, a promised conversation anchored as much in frustration as information sharing. Nathanael's question might have been good natured or frank curiosity, but Philip wisely avoided the conversation with the simple response, "Come and see."

Naming Nathanael as a skeptic does not do the disciple a disservice. The term really respects this type of personality and acknowledges Nathanael's expectations for the Messiah in his hesitations about Nazareth. Sometimes skeptics surface due to powerful negative experiences that leave them honestly suspicious of people's intentions or promises. The number of failed sightings of the Messiah may well have played into the skepticism.

When Nathanael did meet Jesus, our skeptic found himself confronted by something he could not have expected. Jesus greets Nathanael with the phrase, "Here is truly an Israelite in whom there is no deceit!" (John 1:47). The fact that Nathanael's questioning jab did not reflect deceit or treachery is encouraging. However, since some scholars note that John likes to use irony in his book, the observation may have been more playful to a skeptic like Nathanael. In verse 48, Nathanael offers his own question: "Where did you get to know me?" Nathanael could be making an honest inquiry or proffering a fresh challenge to Jesus with an implicit question that was really asking, "Who gives you the right to define me?" Jesus's reply may have startled our skeptic: "I saw you under the fig tree before Philip called you" (v. 48).

The clarity and incomparability of Jesus seeing Nathanael must have been unnerving, since it appears to be insight no one could possess, much less Jesus. It's no wonder, now presented with information that breaks through Nathanael's assumptions, that the disciple declares, "Rabbi, you are the Son of God! You are the King of Israel!" (v. 49). Jesus responds with a question laden with skepticism: "Do you believe because I told you that I saw you under the fig tree?" (v. 50). Perhaps Nathanael, the skeptic, has met his match. Jesus pierces Nathanael's own questioning with an invitation to faith, but he reminds his new disciple that skepticism only goes so far in the realm of belief. Jesus's final statement serves less as a rebuke and more as a promise, one that Jesus will later use for those who believe without seeing (20:29).

Thomas

If Nathanael serves as the skeptic, Thomas might be known as the pessimist in the group. Known as *doubting* Thomas, this disciple may possess an even more negative view than Nathanael ever dreamed of having. Thomas, also "called the Twin" (John 20:24), appears in the lists of the first three gospels (Matt. 10:2-4; Mark 3:16-19; Luke 6:14-16). However, most of the information concerning Thomas surfaces in the Gospel of John. Thomas appears in the story of the resurrection of Lazarus. Jesus, upon hearing of Lazarus's illness, announces a trip to Judea, to Bethany, just outside of Jerusalem. This is a risky proposal. On Jesus's previous trip to Jerusalem, as John 10:22-39 recounts, the Jews attempted to stone him and, when that failed, to arrest him. The idea of returning probably filled the disciples with trepidation, as the exchange between Jesus and the disciples in John 11:7-16 shows. When

Jesus's decision becomes clear, Thomas states, "Let us also go, that we may die with him" (v. 16).

⸺❦⸺

If Nathanael serves as the skeptic, Thomas might be known as the pessimist in the group.

⸺❦⸺

For some commentators, these words may sound courageous, but perhaps what we hear is a bit of resignation and pessimism. Whether wearied from the constant strife revolving around Jesus or from viewing the world as a glass half empty, Thomas sounds like a fatalist as he trudges off to Bethany, toward one of the most powerful stories in Scripture.

Thomas may not be a bitter person but merely someone who needs concrete information lest his concerns overtake his commitments. His devotion to Christ surfaced, as well as his need for clarity, when Jesus told the disciples in the upper room that he was going to go away and prepare a place for them. As Jesus continued, he said, "'And you know the way to the place where I am going.' Thomas said to him, 'Lord, we do not know where you are going. How can we know the way?'" (John 14:4-5). Thomas obviously didn't want to be left behind. However, much like the uncertainty of Jesus's meaning before the journey to Lazarus, Thomas's obedience seemed conditioned by a lack of clear knowledge.[1]

Perhaps the clearest vision of "doubting" Thomas comes after the resurrection when Thomas, questioning Jesus's resurrection, said he would need to touch Jesus's wounds to believe (20:24-25). Thomas was unconvinced by accounts of Jesus's resurrection. Thomas may well reflect the kind of "show me" mentality associated with residents of Missouri, a kind of posture that declares, "I'll believe it when I see it." That same posture is pessimistic. Frank expectations devolve into a mind-set of low expectations that are often rooted in the pain and suffering of past experiences.

So it may well be appropriate that the wounds of Christ's body were needed to alleviate Thomas's doubt. When Jesus appears again to the disciples, with Thomas pointedly in their midst (vv. 26-29), Jesus greets them, saying, "Peace be with you" (v. 26). "Peace" and its Hebrew equivalent, *shālōm*, encompass a range of meaning from a "sense of safety" to a "promise of reconciliation, health, wholeness, friendship, and well-being." In the face of a "doubting" Thomas, and for the sake of all in the room, Jesus offers a full-fledged greeting of peace. Then Jesus invites Thomas not only to see the Savior's wounds but also to touch them. Jesus literally allows Thomas to lay a hand on the wound where a spear pierced his side

---

1. George Lyons and T. Scott Daniels, *John 13–21*, New Beacon Bible Commentary (Kansas City: Beacon Hill Press of Kansas City, 2020), 75.

(John 19:31-37). The spoken promise and the tangible evidence of Jesus's wounds cause Thomas to exclaim, "My Lord and my God!" (20:28). In the face of the tangible brokenness of Jesus, Thomas emerges as a true believer.

Jesus's final response may seem like a chastisement of Thomas's pessimism. Jesus says, "Have you believed because you have seen me? Blessed are those who have not seen and yet have come to believe" (v. 29). However, I think this admonition might be reserved for all of us, not just Thomas (or Nathanael either). Believing is not always easy, especially in difficult times or when the promises of Christ seem too outlandish to skeptics or too wonderful to pessimists. But Jesus reminds us that blessing may come from belief that does not always rely on our knowledge or experience. Blessing comes through faith, a faith we know "is the substance of things hoped for, the evidence of things not seen" (Heb. 11:1, KJV)—a faith that rests on Jesus in spite of everything.

There may be a reason that John also names both Nathanael and Thomas on the boat in the Sea of Galilee (ch. 21). As Peter jumps off the boat to swim toward Jesus, perhaps these two disciples looked down at the net full of fish (v. 8), saw once more the tangible expression of Jesus's power, and then looked at each other. The skeptic and the pessimist, side by side, see the fullness of Christ lived out again. Yes, Peter did drag that fishnet ashore (v. 11), but Nathanael and Thomas sat down at a fire with Jesus, as true believers.

The fellowship of these two skeptics seems to continue into Christian antiquity. Christian tradition strongly suggests that Thomas started the Christian church in India. Some writing also indicates that Thomas later died there by being run through by a spear, reminiscent of Jesus being pierced on the cross.[2] Additionally, Christian tradition asserts that Nathanael may have preached to people in India and translated the book of Matthew into their language.[3] Christian tradition also asserts that Nathanael died as a martyr while serving the people of Ethiopia or Persia.[4] Whether or not these stories prove true, the legacy of these two former skeptics, now true apostles, reminds the church that hard, often critical, questions do matter at times, particularly from those on the margins of life, where easy answers are not always helpful. However, the tangible, concrete love of Christ serves as the best approach to provide a hoped-for response and a hope-filled discipleship for the sake of the kingdom of God.

Joining the Journey

Today, in part due to the influence of the Enlightenment, people adopt a skeptical perspective because they hold the mistaken idea that they possess an absolute control of knowledge. Current skeptics sometimes rest on their intellectual mastery (or fear that their lack of knowledge might be discovered) by constantly questioning the veracity of other people's beliefs and claims. Yet most skepticism rests on the assump-

---

2. *Oxford Dictionary of the Christian Church*, s.v. "Thomas, St."

3. Several sources state that Nathanael merely left a Hebrew copy of the book of Matthew in India, not a translation.

4. *Oxford Dictionary of the Christian Church*, s.v. "Matthew, St."

tions held by skeptics, sometimes good and sometimes bad, in the face of the information they receive. Whether out of pain, or sometimes a sense of intellectual privilege, skeptics know how to turn any question into a challenge.

People who have little to hope for, based on their past, often mute their hopes and dreams for the future. Their critical stance is the result of a world that proves less kind, less promising, less capable of helping these people envision a future where they will flourish. People may not be born with this perspective, but "hard living" drives them to the point of caution. At times they can help congregations learn that many church promises come from a place of privilege. An invitation to submit to Christ may not play well if people have to submit constantly to powerful forces in their lives over which they have little to no control. The invitation to "only believe" feels hollow in a world of shattered promises. The church sometimes needs to encounter pessimistic, matter-of-fact people if only to realize that simple solutions are not that simple after all. The hard questions from people on the margins living hard and painful lives should teach the church that Christ's love needs to be concrete, supportive, and meaningful to many people. The challenge that pessimists offer the church often includes the question that asks, Will the church both *care* for these people and actually *serve* as their protector and advocate? A doubting Thomas, like Nathanael, offers a critical perspective that the body of Christ may well need.

Perhaps that is why John interjects in his writing, following Thomas's encounter with Jesus, the observation that Jesus did many other demonstrable acts, or signs of his divinity, before the disciples. There were a number of other illustrations that portrayed Jesus as a kind of miracle worker. But John insists the stories written in his gospel serve one purpose: "so that you may continue to believe that Jesus is the Messiah, the Son of God, and that through believing you may have life in his name" (John 20:31). That invitation remains open to all, no matter how difficult life might seem or how deep a person's skepticism might be. The invitation to come, see, touch, and know the love of Christ through the life of the church provides a tangible way forward.

Discussion Questions

1. Can you name some reasons why people might grow skeptical or pessimistic over time?

2. Are there positive reasons for people to question or challenge assumptions? Name some circumstances.

3. Why would Jesus's response change Nathanael's perspective so quickly?

4. How would touching the wounds of the resurrected Jesus break down Thomas's pessimism?

5. Why would people need concrete expressions of Jesus's love today? What difference does it make when the church reaches out to people through tangible expressions of love and care?

6. Have you felt skeptical or even pessimistic as a faithful disciple? What has helped you through those moments?

Scripture Studies: Piercing Skeptical Moments

- Wrong Side of the Tracks: John 1:46; 7:41-42, 52
- From Nazareth or from God? John 1:1-18, 29-34
- Show Me: John 20:24-30

five

WHAT'S IN A NAME?
James the Lesser and Judas Thaddeus
(or Fill in the Blank)

✥ We begin this chapter where we left off: on the Sea of Galilee in John 21. This scene is also where we began our journey with Peter in chapter 1. By now we have discussed all of the disciples we might normally expect in the boat: Peter, Andrew, James, John, Nathanael, and Thomas. But just as we think we can leave this passage behind, we discover this odd phrase in verse 2: "Gathered there together were Simon Peter, Thomas called the Twin, Nathanael of Cana in Galilee, the sons of Zebedee, and *two others* of his disciples" (emphasis added). So who were the other two disciples? Yes, Andrew makes sense and perhaps Simon the Zealot, but why didn't John just tell us who the other disciples were? Did he have a memory lapse? Was he protecting the identity of the disciples as if they were in some sort of witness protection program?

Or does it just not matter? For a former journalist like myself, those kinds of "loose threads" often drive me crazy.

However, sometimes my struggle also surfaces when the Gospels offer just enough information to raise more questions, as is the case with the next two disciples of our study. These two individuals appear among the disciples listed in the Gospel of Mark:

Jesus went up on a mountainside and called to him those he wanted, and they came to him. He appointed twelve that they might be with him and that he might send them out to preach and to have authority to drive out demons. These are the twelve he appointed: Simon (to whom he gave the name Peter), James son of Zebedee and his brother John (to them he gave the name Boanerges, which means "sons of thunder"), Andrew, Philip, Bartholomew, Matthew, Thomas, James son of Alphaeus, Thaddaeus, Simon the Zealot and Judas Iscariot, who betrayed him. (3:13-19, NIV)

Mark's version may be the most official listing of the twelve disciples (see also Matt. 10:2-4; Luke 6:14-16; Acts 1:13), but we sometimes have to wonder how James son of Alphaeus and Thaddeus were selected as members of this group over others more well known in the Scriptures.

For instance, we already know the story of Zacchaeus, the "other" tax collector (Luke 19:1-10). Another good candidate, Nicodemus the Pharisee, appears first in John 3:1-21, where he approaches Jesus in the dead of night to find out who Jesus is (a familiar theme for the other disciples). Instead, Jesus offers instruction on the true nature of his calling and the need to be born anew to truly understand the fullness of his role (a theme that plays out across the four gospels and into the book of Acts). Later, we find Nicodemus defending Jesus before the chief priests and Pharisees, arguing that Jesus at least deserves a fair trial (though none of those overseeing this inquest believe anything good can come from Galilee, hearkening back to Nathanael's skepticism in the previous chapter) (7:45-52). Finally, it is Nicodemus who may have been at the final trial of Jesus (18:15-16) and who assists Joseph of Arimathea by providing the customary embalming spices in preparing the body of Jesus for burial (19:39-42).

If actions speak louder than words, then Nicodemus makes more sense than our two disciples in question. However, both James Alphaeus (or James the Lesser) and Thaddeus (who was known by several names) still deserve our consideration for a very special reason.

James the Lesser

What we know of James the Lesser (or James the Younger or James the Minor) revolves around his family relationships. The Gospels identify James as the son of Alphaeus (Luke 6:15), with his mother, Mary (Mark 15:40), and a brother, Joseph or Joses (Matt. 27:56). Except for a few details about his family, there is nothing more mentioned about him in Scripture. Some early church leaders (Jerome in particular) tried to connect James the Lesser with Jesus's brother James through the list of the brothers of Jesus (Matt. 13:55; Mark 6:3): James,

Joseph or Joses, Simon, and Judas. While some Catholic traditions accept this view, others remain unconvinced by the premise. Perhaps the association seems to connect to James the Lesser's mother, Mary, but James the Lesser's mother has her own interesting history. Comparing the accounts of the women at the cross during Jesus's crucifixion creates another interesting "connecting of the dots." As we will see, Mary, the mother of James the Lesser, possibly appears among the women listed at the crucifixion in John 19:25. The list consists of Jesus's mother, Mary, his mother's sister, Mary the wife of Clopas, and Mary Magdalene. Yet James the Lesser's mother also appears in other passages:

- "Mary the mother of James and Joseph" (Matt. 27:56)
- "Mary the mother of James the younger and of Joses" (Mark 15:40), with "James the younger" here also translated "James the less"
- As well as "Mary the mother of James" (Mark 16:1; Luke 24:10)

Confused yet? Sorting out the gospel accounts of men with the name James and of women named Mary takes patience and a little humility.[1] Often Greek sentences leave out key clues, such as punctuation, while also based on the oral accounts of who was present (including John himself, who well may have been focused on Mary, the mother of Jesus, as much as his own mother). Biblical scholars, operat-

---

1. *Oxford Dictionary of the Christian Church*, 3rd ed. (1997), s.v. "Marys in the N.T."

ing more like journalists than storytellers, often try to sort out the genealogies without the benefit of web search engines and ancestry databases, though it's doubtful they could agree with a "gospels.com" genealogy version, even if one appeared. Even the early church fathers could not agree on this question. Many scholars tentatively conclude that Mary of Clopas represents James the Lesser's mother, with Clopas being the Aramaic version of the Greek Alphaeus. However, alternative research suggests that Mary Clopas may just have been another woman, possibly a sister, at the scene.[2]

Sorting out the gospel accounts of men with the name James and of women named Mary takes patience and a little humility.

Leaving Mom aside, the relationship with Dad seems to indicate that James the Lesser was the brother of Levi the

---

2. Richard Bauckham, *Gospel Women: Studies of the Named Women in the Gospels* (Grand Rapids: Eerdmans, 2002), 203-23; Winsome Munroe, "Mary," in *HarperCollins Bible Dictionary*, 658.

tax collector, though this again is questioned by the journal-ist-scholars.[3] While the Gospels celebrate Levi's conversion, as we discussed in chapter 3, there does not seem to be any direct influence by James the Lesser in that story. So why the name James the Lesser or James the Less? Choosing this name might make sense considering the pedigree of the other two Jameses in the Gospels, including James the son of Zebedee (big James) and James the brother of Jesus (brother James), who would become a major leader in the early church in Je-rusalem following his encounter with the resurrected Jesus (see 1 Cor. 15:7; Gal. 2:9) and later, according to the historian Josephus, suffer martyrdom through stoning.

If our James stood between two titans of leaders like "big" James and "brother" James, perhaps the title the "Lesser" (or the "Younger" or "Minor") makes sense. Anyone among the twelve disciples might call him "James Junior" if only to dis-tinguish the relative importance of the two disciples. Being brother to a tax collector does not improve one's station ei-ther. Even claiming youth probably grated against John if he was truly the youngest of the disciples. Our disciple might have felt that James the Lesser proved a fitting compromise. Tradition does indicate that James the Lesser—if we can as-certain that he was truly not the brother of Jesus—ended up being crucified in Persia or Egypt.[4]

---

3. R. E. Nixon, "Alphaeus," in *New Bible Dictionary*, 2nd ed., ed. J. D. Douglas (Leicester, UK: Inter-Varsity Press, 1982), 26.

4. *Oxford Dictionary of the Christian Church*, 3rd ed. (1997), s.v. "James the Less"; Shelton, *Quest for the Historical Apostles*, 205-7.

Judas Thaddeus

When we study Judas Thaddeus, the other disciple of this pair, we experience similar difficulties. We know the Gospels also call Thaddeus by the names Judas, Jude, and Lebbaeus. Ready for more confusion? Jude or Judas occurs six times, in four different contexts:

- "'[Judas] of James,' one of the twelve apostles (Luke 6:16; Acts 1:13)"
- "'Judas (not Judas Iscariot),' apparently an apostle (John 14:22)"
- "The brother of Jesus (Matthew 13:55, Mark 6:3)"
- "The writer of the Epistle of Jude, who identifies himself as 'the brother of James' (Jude 1)"[5]

To further confound the matter, some translations include Matthew 10:3: "Lebbaeus, who was surnamed Thaddaeus" (DARBY). When the biblical scholars, our friendly journalists, wrestle with both early church tradition and the biblical texts, they offer some interesting conclusions (when they can agree).[6] Thaddeus is probably not the Judas who is the brother of Jesus or the writer of the Epistle of Jude, since Luke 6:16 and Acts 1:13 can be translated "Judas son of James" (which is how it reads in the New International Version and the New Revised Version Updated Edition).

5. *Oxford Dictionary of the Christian Church*, 3rd ed. (1997), s.v. "Jude, St."

6. *Oxford Dictionary of the Christian Church*, 3rd ed. (1997), s.v. "Thaddeus, St."

As a young person, I had a number of first cousins and second cousins close to my age. Early in our family gatherings I remember my grandfather struggling with the names of the many different children. I remember him calling "Bobby . . . I mean, Jerry, . . . I mean, Dean, . . . I mean . . . Hey you, come here to Grandpa!" I wonder if Judas, I mean Thaddeus, I mean Lebbaeus, ever experienced something similar?

———⌾———

For Judas Thaddeus or Judas the "Courageous," the nomenclature probably went a long way from distinguishing him from Judas Iscariot.

———⌾———

Judas Thaddeus lived in obscurity as one of the Twelve. He did ask Jesus a question in John 14:22: "Lord, why are you going to reveal yourself only to us and not to the world at large?" (NLT). Judas seemed overly concerned with this question. Christ responded by saying that he would reveal himself to anyone who loved him. Digging into the etymology of the different names (even on Google), we will discover that both

Thaddeus and Lebbaeus probably served as nicknames, with both meaning "a courageous heart," attached to the name Judas.[7] For Judas Thaddeus or Judas the "Courageous," the nomenclature probably went a long way from distinguishing him from Judas Iscariot, who appears in the next chapter. Between James the Lesser and Judas the Courageous, Judas did appear to get the better of the two options.

Joining the Journey

At this point of our exploration you might wonder, "Who cares?" Maybe, like Nicodemus, actions do seem to speak louder than words. From the exploration above we get the impression that if someone were doing an ancestry book, the pages would open and all you would see are a ton of question marks on each page.

Or maybe not. Perhaps, when you opened the first page of the ancestry book, all you would get is one word: "Jesus."

Chasing down the lineage of these two disciples overlooks the fact that what really made them special rests on their relationship with Jesus Christ. They appear in an exclusive list of those closest to Jesus, their names follow Jesus, and their lives (as Judas Thaddeus remarked in John 14:22) revolved around that relationship first and foremost. Regardless of their names, the better nickname for both disciples might well be Jesus Follower.

---

7. *Easton's Bible Dictionary* (1897), s.v. "Lebbaeus," Bible Study Tools, accessed April 5, 2021, https://www.biblestudytools.com /dictionary/lebbaeus/.

The same may be said of many of us. Our heritage may not matter. Perhaps we live quiet lives for Jesus in the way we relate to others and witness quietly through our everyday work and relationships. Maybe the pages of our ancestry book appear pretty bland. But Jesus's assurance to Judas Thaddeus remains Christ's promise to us in John 14:23: "Anyone who loves me will obey my teaching. My Father will love them, and we will come to them and make our home with them" (NIV). Our family tree does not matter because we now live in a new home and reside with a new family, both through Jesus as well as with Jesus, the Father, and the Holy Spirit (vv. 15-21). Being everyday disciples, just ordinary people with ordinary names, is enough when we realize that we follow Jesus and that Jesus defines who we are and to whom we belong.

Discussion Questions

1. Would you want a common name that other people might have or would you prefer a unique name?

2. Why do people confuse the names of children?

3. Would most people feel comfortable living a quiet, somewhat obscure life, or would they want to be remembered for something more?

4. How might the desire for attention hamper or help a person's discipleship?

5. Would you be satisfied if people remembered you primarily as a Jesus follower?

Scripture Studies: Working through Relationships

- Mother of James the Lesser? Matthew 27:56; Mark 16:1; Luke 24:10
- James the Lesser or Someone Else? Matthew 10:3; 13:55; Mark 3:18; Luke 6:15-16; Acts 1:13; 12:17
- Judas (No, the Other Judas) Thaddeus? Matthew 10:2-4; Mark 3:13-19; Luke 6:14-16; John 14:22-23

six

JUDAS ISCARIOT AND SIMON THE ZEALOT
Men of Violence

❖ If the last chapter served as a classic example of journalistic accounting, this final chapter on the twelve disciples serves more as a family story, combining both a cautionary tale and a tale of hope. Our cautionary tale begins with Judas Iscariot. In the listing of the disciples in the Gospel of Mark (3:13-19), he is "Judas Iscariot, who betrayed [Jesus]" (v. 19, NIV). This ignoble introduction (see also Matt. 10:2-4 and Luke 6:14-16) sets the stage for our encounters with Judas along the way, particularly in the Gospel of John.

Judas Iscariot

In John 12, Judas appears in one of the most famous stories surrounding Jesus. Jesus and the disciples find themselves at a dinner in the home of Lazarus, a friend whom Jesus had raised from the dead not long before. Mary, the sister of Lazarus, takes a bottle of costly ointment and breaks it open on Jesus's feet and wipes them with her hair. This humble, spontaneous act of thanksgiving also fills the entire home with the aroma of this unadulterated gift of pure nard. At that point, the tenderness of the moment must have seemed palpable. But then John continues:

> But one of his disciples, Judas Iscariot, who was later to betray him, objected, "Why wasn't this perfume sold and the money given to the poor? It was worth a year's wages." He did not say this because he cared about the poor but because he was a thief; as keeper of the money bag, he used to help himself to what was put into it.
>
> "Leave her alone," Jesus replied. "It was intended that she should save this perfume for the day of my burial. You will always have the poor among you [Deut. 15:11], but you will not always have me." (Vv. 4-8, NIV)

Mark 14:3-9 carries a similar story in the home of Simon the Leper. An unidentified woman breaks a jar of perfume, pours it on Jesus's head, and gets the same rebuke, but from "some" of the disciples (v. 4). From John's passage we begin to sense what, to many, appears to be the man who might be the treasurer for Jesus's disciples. A similar passage, John 13:29, carries those assumptions and suggests Judas collects support for the twelve disciples and for distributing the same to the poor. However, John takes time to state that Judas is also a thief and, by implication, a liar (12:6).

Left with this character reference, we might believe this is a clear-cut case of a genuine "bad guy" that managed to sneak his way into the inner company of Jesus. Yet our total understanding of Judas, the betrayer, comes with some speculation. For instance, scholars (those reporters we discussed) have struggled with his last name, Iscariot. The term appears to be a derivation of "man of Kerioth," which may have been a Judean township (or cluster of small towns) or even just a suburban township. The name does imply that Judas did not reside in Galilee where the other disciples found their home. Even the name Judas points to a likely Judean background, so he may well have come to symbolize the popular movement around Jesus as the Savior moved from the ministry around Galilee to ministry in Judea. So the names imply Judas Iscariot may have been a late member of the band.[1]

Some scholars, like members of the family protecting the proverbial rogue nephew, try to rehabilitate Judas's reputation regardless of John's fiery depiction of the disciple. These scholars argue that Judas actually acted as a friend, trying to assist or force Jesus to become the Messiah most people anticipated—that is, a Messiah who would take back power from the Romans and return the Jewish people to God's rule. This view of the anticipated Messiah (or Savior-Warrior) dominated popular Jewish belief and could well be both what James and John first expected as they hoped to sit at the right and left hand of Jesus. Judas, rather than a thief, really served as a cautious treasurer, perhaps with mixed motives, hoping at

---

1. *Oxford Dictionary of the Christian Church*, 3rd ed. (1997), s.v. "Judas Iscariot."

best to "introduce" Jesus to the Sanhedrin in a quiet manner or at worse to force an arrest to start the revolution (or perhaps to do both).[2] Regardless of the speculation, if John's Gospel provides the final interpretation, then Jesus admitted Judas to the Twelve for a specific reason and not because of the disciple's natural ability.

In John 6:1-14, a very troubling encounter occurs between Jesus and the people after Jesus feeds the five thousand and is pursued by the crowd, apparently hoping for more bread (vv. 22-24). Jesus confronts the crowd with a real challenge to accept him as the bread of life. He declares that true life comes from the "bread from heaven" (v. 32; referring to himself, instead of the manna of Exod. 16:1-35). Jesus concludes by saying that this life will come from eating his flesh and drinking his blood (John 6:53-59), probably a foreshadowing of Jesus's message to the twelve disciples in the upper room later. The "followers" and even other disciples, probably appalled and dispirited, then turn away in the face of this "hard teaching" (v. 60, NIV; see vv. 60-66).

---

2. William Klassen, *Judas: Betrayer or Friend of Jesus?* (Minneapolis: Fortress Press, 1996); Marvin Meyer, *Judas: The Definitive Collection of Gospels and Legends about the Infamous Apostle of Jesus* (New York: HarperOne, 2007). Much of this argument really rests on the meaning behind one Greek word that many of the Gospels translate as "betray." The apostle Paul uses the same word to describe both the "delivering" or "handing over" of Jesus sacrificially for our salvation and the "handing over" or "betraying" of Jesus in the recounting of the Lord's Supper (Gal. 2:19-20; Rom. 8:31-32; 1 Cor. 11:23-24). Simply put, by "delivering" (the same word as "betraying") Jesus, Judas hoped the revolution would begin.

Left with only the Twelve, Jesus turns his challenge on them, asking if they, too, want to leave. Once again, Simon Peter speaks, probably with the same candor we have observed before: "Lord, to whom shall we go? You have the words of eternal life. We have come to believe and to know that you are the Holy One of God" (vv. 68-69, NIV). Even during this moment of allegiance John reminds us of a traitor in their midst through Jesus's answer to Peter and the Twelve. "Jesus replied, 'Have I not chosen you, the Twelve? Yet one of you is a devil!' (He meant Judas, the son of Simon Iscariot, who, though one of the Twelve, was later to betray him)" (vv. 70-71, NIV).

Whatever the motivation, the time line of Judas's actions provides a troubling picture. Judas approaches the high priests and leaders, probably in the Sanhedrin, to negotiate "handing over" Jesus for an agreed price of thirty pieces of silver. Then Judas begins to look for an opportunity (Matt. 26:14-16; Mark 14:10-11; Luke 22:3-6). Judas is among the Twelve as Jesus washes their feet and begins to predict his betrayal (John 13:1-20). Jesus makes it clear that one person will betray him during the Last Supper. Each disciple, one by one, asks if he was the betrayer. Jesus verbally reveals Judas Iscariot, as that disciple accepts from Jesus bread from the cup, the first institution of the Lord's Supper (vv. 26-27; Matt. 26:20-25; Mark 14:17-21; Luke 22:14, 22-23).

Even when the Twelve gather in the upper room, we see a picture of both joy and sorrow. John provides the most intimate portrayal and makes clear that a troubled Jesus knows of Judas's betrayal. Judas's acceptance signals (to John) Satan's invasion of Judas's spirit. Jesus releases Judas with the words "What you are about to do, do quickly" before the confused and mystified disciples (John 13:27, NIV). Reading the depth of Jesus's teaching from John 14–17, one realizes just how much of Jesus Christ's love and comfort Judas completely misses as he leaves to alert the authorities that the time is at hand. The only time Jesus mentions Judas occurs during Christ's prayer for God's protection and for the unity of the disciples. Jesus acknowledges that Judas, this "son of perdition," must betray the Savior according to the Scriptures (John 17:12, KJV). Judas no longer resides within the fellowship of the disciples.

Judas betrays Jesus in the garden of Gethsemane with a greeting, but also a kiss (Matt. 26:46-50; Luke 22:47-49; John 18:1-9). What seems to be an innocent act unleashes the violent interrogation and ultimate crucifixion of Jesus. A simple act, so seemingly insignificant, overcomes many other instances where crowds tried to assault or arrest the Son of God. The same gesture also leads to Judas's own unraveling.

Regardless of his initial motivations, Judas's actions lead to Jesus experiencing a violent ending.

Filled with regret for his action, Judas tries to return the thirty pieces of silver to the high priests. When the priests refuse the money, Judas casts the coins onto the floor of the temple. The priests, not wanting "blood money" in the temple treasury, buy the "potter's field" for the burial of foreigners (not wanting to even tarnish the Jewish dead) (Matt. 27:6-7). Matthew notes that this symbolic act fulfills one of Jeremiah's prophecies, perhaps closing the loop of Jesus's assertion that Judas's act would fulfill Scripture (vv. 3-10).

Judas's own death takes on a grisly scene. Comparing the two accounts of Judas's death in Matthew 27 and in Acts 1, we find that Judas takes his own life by hanging (Matt. 27:5) and that apparently his body remains suspended until it decomposes enough to fall to the ground and burst open (Acts 1:18). This gruesome ending marks the end of one of the Twelve, a unique group, as Peter's comments indicate when they choose Judas's replacement (vv. 15-22). Readers should recognize that the two men chosen as candidates, Joseph (also known as Barsabbas or Justus) and Matthias, lived as part of the disciples from John the Baptist's first declaration of Jesus as the Lamb of God (John 1:29) to Jesus's resurrection. Matthias joins the inner circle of the Twelve that Judas abandoned (Acts 1:21-26).

This painful, sometimes complex story indeed serves as a cautionary tale inside the family. Regardless of his initial motivations, Judas's actions lead to Jesus experiencing a violent ending. One wonders when exactly Judas tried to return the silver to the high priests. In Matthew's time line it follows

Jesus's interrogation by the high priests, Jesus's first beating, and his condemnation to death (Matt. 26:57-68). Was Judas in the crowd? During the death verdict, did Judas remember the words Jesus spoke in the garden of Gethsemane? "Now the hour is at hand, and the Son of Man is betrayed into the hands of sinners. Get up, let us be going. Look, my betrayer is at hand" (vv. 45b-46).

We do know that Judas's last name, Iscariot, would later be associated with the term "assassin" (Latin, *sicarii*) and describe generations of violent men that followed him.

Simon the Zealot

Perhaps the sobering reflections around Judas Iscariot's life prepare us for one final disciple, bearing one final story of hope. At first glance, the life of Simon the Zealot seems like a pretty small tale compared to that of Judas Iscariot. However, as we learned already, there is sometimes power in the names of the disciples when we pause to look.

The information around Simon the Zealot really seems quite similar to our two disciples from the previous chapter, James the Lesser and Judas Thaddeus. We know he is counted as one of the Twelve in Matthew 10:4; Mark 3:18; Luke 6:15; and Acts 1:13. Along with the Twelve, he also was sent on a mission: "These twelve Jesus sent out with the following instructions: 'Do not go among the Gentiles or enter any town of the Samaritans. Go rather to the lost sheep of Israel. As you go, proclaim this message: "The kingdom of heaven has come near." Heal the sick, raise the dead, cleanse those who have leprosy, drive out demons. Freely you have received; freely give'" (Matt. 10:5-8, NIV; see also Mark 6:6-13 and Luke 9:7-13).

The context of this mission is the first time Simon is mentioned in Matthew (and in the New Testament), but this merely means that Simon was willing to follow Jesus's mission into the world. In a similar manner, Simon joined the other disciples at the Last Supper (26:20). He also listened with the other disciples in Galilee as Jesus presented the Great Commission: "And Jesus came and said to them, 'All authority in heaven and on earth has been given to me. Go therefore and make disciples of all nations, baptizing them in the name of the Father and of the Son and of the Holy Spirit and teaching them to obey everything that I have commanded you. And remember, I am with you always, to the end of the age'" (28:18-20).

So we find Simon the Zealot, much like James the Lesser or Judas Thaddaeus, merely as one of the Twelve, with no other contribution. Why conclude our study of the Twelve with this disciple? Probably because of his name. To be certain, Simon the "Cananean" (Aramaic for "zealot") probably needed to be distinguished from Simon Peter, our first member of the Twelve. However, instead of taking a family name (Zebedee, Alphaeus, Bartholomew, to name three), Simon seems to be carrying the specific designation of zealot.[3]

---

3. *Oxford Dictionary of the Christian Church*, 3rd ed. (1997), s.v. "Simon, St., 'the Less.'"

At the time of Jesus, the term "zealot" might designate one of two specific groups of people. The first seemed to refer to those particularly zealous for the Torah, or law of Moses. The apostle Paul reflects this kind of zealotry within his own background, as Saul, in Acts 22:3 and Galatians 1:14. This kind of zealous behavior probably served Saul-Paul well at the stoning of Stephen (Acts 7:58) or in arresting of Jesus's followers in Jerusalem (8:1-3) or on his journey to arrest Jesus's followers in Damascus (9:1-3). This kind of zealotry carried punitive power.

The other group of people known as the Zealots date back to AD 6, when a different historical figure known as Judas the Galilean led a revolt against Rome, probably over the paying tribute to a pagan emperor in Rome. Zealots seem to appear regularly as an ongoing Jewish resistance from that time to AD 66 and the beginning of another revolt that culminated in the final capture of Masada in AD 74.[4] This kind of unrest probably explains Pilate killing a number of Galileans in Luke 13:1-3. Some scholars consider Zealots the fourth major political group—that is, Jewish nationalists orchestrating a long running skirmish with Roman authorities, a movement that Jesus seems to refuse to join in his own ministry (Mark 12:14-17).

Apparently, Simon chose a term that, whether as enforcer or terrorist, bore a deep association with both religious fervor and violence. Yet Simon chose to follow the Prince of Peace,

---

4. F. F. Bruce, "Zealot," in *New Bible Dictionary*, 1273-74; Pheme Perkins, "Zealot," in *HarperCollins Bible Dictionary*, 1237.

the one who taught Simon that he was blessed when meek, peaceful, persecuted, and reviled for the kingdom of God (Matt. 5:1-12). Simon would hear Jesus's first mission statement calling him to manifest Jesus's own miraculous power as a member of the Twelve, and he would later stand to hear Jesus give him a final commission to "make disciples" (28:19). This man, whose previous life might well be filled with political violence against Rome, inherited the Gospel dedicated to peace and reconciliation for all the world. Simon's "zeal" would reflect the love of God and neighbor. Whatever violent passion of the past, Simon's chosen name came to represent a different future as a disciple.

Simon demonstrated that no matter how violent a past, no matter how questionable the character, life with the Savior can provide redemption and hope.

If you search, you will find some speculation about what happened to Simon. Tradition says that after preaching on the west coast of Africa, Simon went to England, where he ended up being crucified in AD 74. Whether this is true or not, we can just rest in knowing that Simon demonstrated that no matter how violent a past, no matter how questionable the character, life with the Savior can provide redemption and hope. Sometimes our legacy finds its place with Jesus, and the possibilities may be far more than we imagine.

Joining the Journey

The stories of the twelve disciples could end on the terrible tale of Judas Iscariot, if only to ask the hard questions of how our own efforts, even when well intended, might go terribly wrong. Could any of us, even as dedicated disciples of Jesus, find ourselves so focused on our own interpretation of Jesus that we risk damaging the very Christ we are called to follow? Do we make small compromises (either in asserting our will or succumbing to temptation) to the point that we create incredible pain and suffering in other people's lives? How might our mixed motives wind up taking us down a wrong path even if we think we can cover up our own selfish desires? How often do people see us for who we really are when we push our agenda? Judas, as a cautionary tale, forces us to take a sober look in the mirror and take serious account of our motives and behaviors. How will our legacy be remembered in the family of God?

However, the final story rests with another disciple, one whose very description reflected a violent path—a path now rejected, perhaps even redeemed, by choosing to follow Jesus.

This story provides hope that regardless of our previous lives, we can find a new identity in Jesus Christ. How often might we have a name that, in another life, might have been associated with violence, theft, treachery, or some other sin that, if public, would brand us forever? Would we be willing to see that name reshaped, redeemed, by Jesus Christ? Perhaps we do not need to place our shortcomings, our sin, on display. However, when people see the change in our lives from becoming disciples of Christ, they may acknowledge not only our former selves but also the kind of life we have now chosen. May it be so for us all.

Discussion Questions

1. Can you think of circumstances when people might act with mixed motives to serve both a cause and themselves?

2. Can decisions go terribly wrong? Even when we want the best for someone or some circumstance, what might happen to change the outcome to create more harm than good?

3. Are people honest with themselves when it comes to their motivations? Why or why not?

4. Can you think of someone who came out of a sinful life to live as a disciple of Jesus? What happened in that person's life and to the lives of people around that person?

5. When you consider your legacy, what story do you hope it will tell?

Scripture Studies: Questionable Character

- John's Vision of Judas Iscariot: John 6:70-71; 12:4-8; 13:2, 27-29
- Matthew's Account of Judas's Betrayal: Matthew 26:1-5, 14-16, 20-25, 47-56
- Judas's Final Fate: Matthew 27:1-10; Acts 1:18-20

seven

SERVANT LEADERS
Mary, Martha, and Mary Magdalene

❖ No book on the disciples of Jesus need end with the twelve disciples of the inner circle. Yes, the Twelve were important, if only by their clear demarcation. However, in the previous chapter, we observed that Joseph (also known as Barsabbas or Justus) and Matthias both followed Jesus from his early ministry all the way to his ascension. This dedication qualified them to replace Judas Iscariot (Acts 1:21-26). We find other nameless disciples, or at least followers, in John 6:60-66. These depictions of disciples—both individuals and large groups—remind us that other people followed Jesus and were sent by Jesus. These other disciples included a special cohort, the women around Jesus.

It is almost impossible to ignore the influence of women in and around Jesus, beginning with Jesus's lineage prior to his birth in Matthew. Matthew 1:1-16 includes five women in his annotated genealogy: Tamar (see Gen. 38); Rahab (Josh. 2); Ruth (the book of Ruth); the wife of Uriah, which some associate with Bathsheba (2 Sam. 11–12); and Mary, the mother of Jesus. Scholars note that all of these women, except Mary, possessed either Gentile origins or at least some Gentile connections. The women appear to be people on the margins of power, but they also serve as major characters in key stories in Scripture.[1]

The presence of women throughout Jesus's crucifixion and resurrection story remains a persistent reminder of their importance.

Jesus is identified as Mary's, not Joseph's, son in Matthew 1:18-25. Obviously Mary, the mother of Jesus, also occupies a large history in the church today. However, other women figure prominently in Jesus's story, such as Mary's relative Elizabeth, the wife of Zechariah and the mother of John the Baptist (Luke 1:4-45). Also the prophet Anna (like Simeon in 2:25-35) provides a vision that might represent the first public declaration of Jesus's mission to others (vv. 36-38). Other

---

1. Bauckham, *Gospel Women*, 17-46.

women, such as the aristocratic patrons Joanna and Susanna, appear at key junctures of Luke's Gospel (8:1-3; 24:10), providing economic resources for Jesus's ministry and proclaiming that Jesus had risen from the grave.[2] Actually, the presence of women throughout Jesus's crucifixion and resurrection story remains a persistent reminder of their importance.[3]

So naming women as disciples should not come as a surprise. However, unlike previous lessons, our "pairing" this time will involve three women, the sisters Mary and Martha and then Mary Magdalene. Mary and Martha do not occur often in the New Testament, but their names remain well known. Although contemporary understandings of their significance to the early church have been eclipsed by the scholarly preoccupation with Mary Magdalene, they were highly revered by ancient Christians, with Mary, the sister of Martha, committing one act (the pouring of costly ointment on Jesus's feet mentioned in the previous chapter) that sets her apart from many other women (John 12:1-8).

Mary and Martha

The most famous story about the sisters appears in Luke 10:38-42, but they also figure prominently in John 11:1–12:8 and in many postbiblical traditions. We find Jesus visiting the house of Martha in Luke 10:38-42, though a similar story in John 12:1 sets this encounter at the house of Lazarus (who

---

2. Ibid., 109-202.
3. Ibid., 257-310.

is not mentioned in Luke's story). Martha, "distracted by her many tasks," appears upset with her sister, Mary, who sits at Jesus's feet listening to him (Luke 10:40). Martha asks Jesus to encourage Mary to rise and help her. Jesus replies, "Martha, Martha, you are worried and distracted by many things, but few things are needed—indeed only one. Mary has chosen the better part, which will not be taken away from her" (vv. 41-42).

Undoubtedly, many of us have heard sermons (or read books) about the contrast between the sisters (and Jesus's seeming rebuke). Usually, adoration and contemplation seem the better option when contrasted with the way of Martha, whose bias toward action may come closer to the manner of Peter, the lead disciple. However, whether we possess a heart like Mary or are constantly active like Martha, we must not miss the main point. Biblical scholar Mary Ann Beavis observes that Martha may seem to be a homemaker frustrated with her less-than-diligent sister, but there is more going on. To begin with, in Jesus's admonishment, while directing attention to the crucial matter of "his presence," he does not explain what he means by the phrase "one thing . . . the better part." Also, Martha is not depicted doing work around the house but as a host, which certainly is "'service' (Greek: *diakonian*)." Dr. Beavis continues:

> By contrast, Luke depicts Mary as a disciple sitting at Jesus' feet. Both women are engaged in different aspects of ministry, or ways of following Jesus and his teachings. The story illustrates how householders should treat visiting teachers. Mary Stromer Hanson observes that it isn't even

clear that Mary is in the house *with* Martha and Jesus; possibly, Martha's complaint is that Mary's discipleship has taken her away from home.[4]

Overall, the normal presentations of these two women in popular books and sermons may not really reflect the depth of their discipleship.[5] Both women stand as proven disciples and servant leaders in the way they demonstrated their faith.

As noted previously, John also includes the story of the two sisters when Jesus raises their brother Lazarus from the dead (John 11:1–12:8). John makes it clear that Jesus loves both the brother and the sisters alike (11:5). Scholar Mary Beavis observes that this family seems to contain the only people mentioned as being loved by name in John's Gospel. Both women figure significantly in the story: Martha confesses that Jesus is the Messiah (v. 27), and Mary's tears prompt Jesus to raise Lazarus (vv. 28-44). In gratitude, Mary anoints Jesus's feet with perfume at a banquet, but a banquet where, once again, "Martha served," perhaps even as the default leader or head of the household (12:2). The two women really stand side by side as active participants, which could easily classify them as disciples of Jesus.

---

4. Mary Ann Beavis, "Mary and Martha," Bible Odyssey, accessed March 27, 2021, https://www.bibleodyssey.org:443/people/main-articles/mary-and-martha.

5. Mary Stromer Hanson, *The New Perspective on Mary and Martha: Do Not Preach Mary and Martha Again Until You Read This!* (Eugene, OR: Wipf and Stock, 2013).

Mary Magdalene

As mentioned earlier, the women in the Gospels appear most prominently at Jesus's crucifixion and resurrection. Mary Magdalene is the one name consistent in all four gospels of the New Testament.[6] According to Mark and Luke, Mary Magdalene's discipleship probably followed after Jesus cast out of her seven demons (Mark 16:9; Luke 8:2). Whether Mary experienced an actual exorcism or suffered from a spiritual illness, she apparently chose to join Jesus rather than remain behind.

As noted earlier, the Gospel of Luke provides insights into Mary's role in Jesus's life and ministry, listing her among "some women who had been cured of evil spirits and infirmities" but also alongside the women economically supporting the disciples in ministry (8:2; see vv. 1-3). Mary seems to be in an inner circle of leadership quite unique in supporting the other disciples. Mary joined a group of women who traveled with Jesus and the twelve disciples, "proclaiming the good news of the kingdom of God" (v. 1, NIV).

Unfortunately, thanks to some of the struggles to discern the many "Marys" in the Bible (mentioned in ch. 5), Mary Magdalene fell victim to popular conflations that tarnished her reputation, from the stories of the early church to the story lines of modern rock operas. To begin with, "Magdalene" is not a surname but identifies the place Mary came from:

---

6. Bauckham, *Gospel Women*, 298-99.

Magdala, a city in Galilee, located in the northernmost region of ancient Palestine (now northern Israel). However, as time passed, the family stories told about our servant-leader Mary were not as kind as those told about the other disciples.

Magdalene walked along as a true outsider to the family of Jesus, and yet she was the first evangelist of Jesus's resurrection. No disciple, not one, bears this place of privilege in the "good news" of the gospel story.

Early church leaders conflated Mary Magdalene with other women mentioned in the Bible, including an unnamed woman, identified in the Gospel of Luke as a sinner, who bathes Jesus's feet with her tears, dries them, and puts ointment on them (Luke 7:37-38), as well as Mary of Bethany, who also appears in Luke (8:38-42).[7] So instead of viewing Mary Magdalene as

---

7. *Oxford Dictionary of the Christian Church*, 3rd ed. (1997), s.v. "Mary Magdalene."

a healed and dedicated disciple, Christians were led to believe that she was a repentant prostitute (or even a woman caught in adultery in John 8:1-11). In AD 591, Pope Gregory the Great solidified this misunderstanding in a sermon: "She whom Luke calls the sinful woman, whom John calls Mary [of Bethany], we believe to be the Mary from whom seven devils were ejected according to Mark."[8] The conflation of these roles does a disservice not only to Mary of Bethany but also to Mary Magdalene, the very woman who would stand beside Mary, the mother of Jesus, at the foot of the cross (John 19:25).

Perhaps the most compelling evidence occurs *after* the death of Jesus, when Mary appears in all four gospels (Matt. 28:1-15; Mark 16:1-13; Luke 24:1-12; John 20:1-18). William Willimon, Methodist preacher, bishop, and chaplain of Duke University, preached a sermon where he recounted that the remaining eleven disciples probably found themselves terrified that morning. They were likely seen as dissidents, were susceptible to arrest, and were crushed knowing that with three days past since the crucifixion (according to Jewish custom), Jesus's spirit surely had departed his body. Frightened, discouraged, in the gloom just before the break of dawn, what do the disciples do? Willimon sardonically says, "Well, they tell the ladies, 'Why don't you just go on and meander down to the tomb and then let us know what is going on.'"[9] According

8. David Van Biema and Lisa McLaughlin, "Mary Magdalene: Saint or Sinner?" *Time*, August 11, 2003, 52-55.

9. William H. Willimon, sermon delivered March 1991.

to the passages, Mary Magdalene traveled in pretty auspicious company, including Mary the mother of Jesus. Magdalene walked along as a true outsider to the family of Jesus, and yet she was the first evangelist of Jesus's resurrection. No disciple, not one, bears this place of privilege in the "good news" of the gospel story.

Amazingly, there is also strong evidence that Mary's encounter at the empty tomb includes a direct encounter with the risen Lord. John 20:11-18 recounts a tender meeting reminiscent of Jesus with Peter by the Sea of Galilee. Following the departure of Peter and John from the empty tomb, Mary enters and finds two angels seated where Jesus's body once lay. Still thinking that someone had taken Jesus's body, Mary's grief seems palatable as she implores both the angels and then, weeping, encounters a person standing outside the tomb whom she believes to be a gardener. Her plaintive appeal for information stops when she hears a familiar voice speak her name. Mary turns and says, "Teacher!" Mary's joy at seeing Jesus is that of the disciple she has been all along. Jesus does not allow Mary to reach out to him (due to some condition associated with his transforming, resurrected body) but sends her to tell the disciples. The passage concludes with a simple statement: "Mary Magdalene went to the disciples with the news: 'I have seen the Lord!' And she told them that he had said these things to her" (v. 18, NIV). When we proclaim on Easter Sunday "He is risen," you can almost hear Mary say, "Yes, that's right. He is!"

Joining the Journey

Any book on the disciples ultimately fails if the contents do not take seriously the faithfulness and servant leadership of those women who literally walked with their Lord and Savior. We can learn deeply from these women of faith, not only in their humanity but also in their devotion. Both Martha, with her independence and bias toward action, and her sister Mary, whose devotion and outright generosity exceeded normal expectations, provide models for us all. Yes, and we can ponder the special qualities of Mary the mother of Jesus and the other women who stood behind John the Baptist and the twelve disciples.

However, Mary Magdalene, whose healing remains a miracle unto itself, stands with the inner circle of Peter, James, and John. Mary Magdalene embodies a gospel testimony, as an eyewitness to the crucifixion, as the first person to encounter the resurrected body of Jesus, and as the first evangelist of the good news. In our everyday life, who better to emulate than Mary Magdalene, the one who even sees the resurrected Lord as her teacher. Would we be willing to do no less?

Women often "disappear" in the telling of the gospel story, even more than James the Lesser and Judas Thaddeus. Yet these women provide some of the most powerful stories of discipleship in Scripture, in church history, and even today. Hearing the dedication and leadership of such women, whether they be inclined to action, contemplative in nature, or just clear in their willingness to witness to the resurrected Jesus, remains our challenge and responsibility for the sake of today's church.

Discussion Questions

1. How often do you hear about women leading in the church either from the Scriptures or from church history?

2. Why are women in the New Testament often excluded when discussing the disciples?

3. Can you name some exceptional women leaders in the world today? How about in the church today?

4. Do women have an equal chance for leadership in our churches? Why or why not?

5. Whether you are female or male, how might you support women disciples in the church to be all that Jesus calls them to be?

Studies: Women Making a Difference

- Story of Lazarus: John 11:1–12:8
- Mary Magdalene at the Cross: Matthew 27:55-56; Mark 15:40-47; Luke 23:49; John 19:25
- Mary Magdalene and the Resurrected Jesus: Matthew 28:1-10; Mark 16:1-8; Luke 24:10; John 20:1-18

eight

A MISSIONAL COMMAND AND CAUTION
The Seventy-Two and the Good Samaritans

❖ So far we have journeyed with specific people who we know to be disciples. Some disciples obviously dominate the conversation, such as Peter, James and John, Judas Iscariot, and Mary Magdalene. Others remain less prominent but helpful reminders of Jesus's ability to reach out through the disciples' differences, devotion, or commitment and, for some, just through their relationship with the Lord. We may have found ourselves, our challenges, and our potential gifts through examining their lives. Yet could there be a larger purpose for all of us as disciples? If so, what might that be?

We could jump to the book of Acts for clues, finding stories not only of the apostles but also of Saul (later Paul), Barnabas, and Stephen. We could also find cautionary tales, such as that of Ananias and Sapphira, to mirror the tortured life of Judas Iscariot. We would even find little known participants, such as Rhoda, a little girl greeting Peter as he enters a room of faithful believers (12:12-18). However, such a strategy (while worth perhaps another book) fails to remind us that we also are like the disciples, not the apostles, with our own challenges to find and follow Jesus in and through our humanity. Before we can "claim" our excellence as apostles, we need to better learn to live and walk with Jesus like the disciples.

So could the Gospels provide a clue to our purpose and our calling as disciples? Should discipleship merely be walking *with* Jesus so we can learn *from* Jesus? Or does Jesus expect us to do something based on our relationship with him? Mary Magdalene might provide a clue, along with Jesus's command to the Twelve in Matthew 10:5-8, which we encountered in chapter 6. A quick rereading of that passage may make all of us a little queasy if this is our missional command as well. Heal the sick, including leprosy? Drive out demons? Raise the dead? These are tall marching orders for everyday disciples. But Jesus did leave another set of "missional instructions" addressed to a larger set of disciples, which might help us find our way.

Sending of the Seventy (Two)

Luke 10:1-16 provides a template that might surprise us. However, before proceeding to unpack the meaning of this passage, we probably need to explore a little more of the mission assigned to the Twelve while also examining some of the variations behind our passage.[1]

Other than the phenomenal calling to heal and perform exorcisms as evidence of the Twelve's ministry, the commission seemed to rely on the presence or lack of hospitality.

Unlike Jesus's commission to the Twelve in Matthew 10:5-8, the tenor of Jesus's command in Luke 10 appears to come closer to the same commission in Mark 6:7-13 and Luke 9:1-6, which may prove important as we proceed. In those passages, Jesus also commands the Twelve to carry no more than needed, with no bread, no bag, no cash, and no extra

---

1. David A. Neale, *Luke 9–24*, New Beacon Bible Commentary (Kansas City: Beacon Hill Press of Kansas City, 2013), 56-71; Walter J. Harrelson, ed., *The New Interpreter's Study Bible: New Revised Standard Version with the Apocrypha* (Nashville: Abingdon Press, 2003). Most study notes come from either David Neale or *The New Interpreter's Study Bible* notes.

clothes (Mark 6:8-9; Luke 9:3-4). In addition, the Twelve were to enter homes that offered respite, but they were to respond to those that rejected them by using an ancient Near Eastern custom of shaking the dust off their feet as a kind of "testimony" against those who refused to be hospitable (Mark 6:10-11; Luke 9:4-5). Otherwise, they were to announce the good news of the kingdom (Luke 9:6) while calling people to repent (Mark 6:12), mirroring Jesus's own words at the start of his ministry (1:14-15). So other than the phenomenal calling to heal and perform exorcisms as evidence of the Twelve's ministry, the commission seemed to rely on the presence or lack of hospitality.

Also, scholars have often wondered whether Jesus called seventy-two disciples or just seventy. The different numbers can be attributed to variations in the earliest manuscript extracts we have of Luke's Gospel. Some Bible translations prefer the lower number, and others the higher. Looking for a numerical significance may prove difficult (though some biblical scholars claim the number seventy-two represents the total number of nations in Genesis 10, implying a global outreach), but suffice it to say that the actual number may be less important.[2] People do wonder where these seventy-two disciples might have come from. In the previous two chapters, we took note of other disciples who probably joined Jesus as early as the beginning of his ministry in Galilee. Some may have been the direct recipients of the mission of the Twelve—namely,

---

2. Harrelson, *New Interpreter's Study Bible*, note on Luke 10:1.

people who were healed and believed the message of repentance (which John the Baptist had been preaching prior to Jesus [Mark 1:1-8]) and the promise of the kingdom of God. So, like many of us, they may well have been believers following after Jesus. The rest of the "mission statement" from Jesus in Luke 10:1-16 continues with the following "stipulations":

First, don't go alone (v. 1). The disciples were sent "two by two," reminiscent of Jewish law that required two witnesses for a convincing testimony and in anticipation of the pairs of apostles, such as Barnabas and Paul, in the book of Acts (NIV). However, this time the disciples were going to the same towns Jesus would visit later, so they also went as ambassadors of Christ.

Second, you are a necessary worker, but don't expect it to be easy (vv. 2-4). The language of a full harvest and the need for laborers remind us that the disciples' efforts in the kingdom prove essential. However, Jesus's admonition that on their journey they would be "like lambs among wolves" (v. 3, NIV; see also Matt. 10:16) spoke to the implicit danger of the journey. The admonishment not to carry additional supplies (like the command to the Twelve) and to avoid the delay of greeting others on the way is a reminder of the personal challenges and demands of fulfilling the mission.

Third, spread peace and be respectful (vv. 5-7). Unlike the message given to the Twelve, Jesus adds the new commandment that they were to enter a household by first extending peace, or *shālōm*, to the household. This clear declaration also served as an invitation to share peacefully with one another and, if rejected, to graciously withdraw. The gracious sharing of meals proved essential in Jewish culture (remember when Jesus dined with others, such as Matthew's tax collectors and sinners). Jesus wanted the disciples to partake of the hospitality of others without capitalizing on it by moving from house to house for better offerings.

Fourth, make a difference, but remember your witness centers on the kingdom of God (vv. 8-10). Jesus expands his message from the household to the whole community but reminds the disciples to maintain a respectful courteousness. The commission to serve as a healing presence may seem daunting (but the same command later motivated Christians to establish the first hospitals).[3] However, the command underscores the expectation that people would be changed physically, as well as spiritually, by the presence of the disciples. Yet even when making a physical difference in people's lives, the disciples were to recognize that their work merely served as an expression of, and an invitation to see, the kingdom of God at work.

Fifth, when in doubt, speak your peace and move on (vv. 10-12). Hospitality at a community level probably proved riskier than moving from house to house. Jesus seems to imply that sometimes disciples would find their mission totally thwarted by the overall challenge of culture and custom. What were the disciples to do? Like the mission of the Twelve, Jesus instruct-

3. L. Gregory Jones, *Christian Social Innovation: Renewing Wesleyan Witness* (Nashville: Abingdon Press, 2016).

ed them to "shake the dust" from their feet. Trying to unpack the full meaning of this phrase probably takes more space than possible in this study. Remember that disciples walked in open sandals, when they had them, on dirt roads shared by animals and other travelers. A basic act of hospitality in Middle Eastern culture entailed washing the feet of people as they entered a home (as Jesus did in the upper room in John 13:1-20). Often, to this day, to show the bottom of one's foot to a person in the Middle East serves as a personal affront, given what might lie on the bottom of that foot.

Shaking the "dust" from a foot might represent the reality that the disciples did not receive the reciprocal hospitality offered above, and leaving the "dust behind" might be a ceremonial expression of leaving behind the "unclean" thoughts and actions presented to them. The meaning could be even more confrontational, but this common practice (Acts 13:51; 18:6) seems to represent a way to "move on." Yet even when leaving, the disciples' missional mandate to remind the town of the inevitability of the kingdom of God remains. Even in the face of a town filled with inhospitable people, they could still offer the good news, which Jesus himself announced and embodied in his message and ministry.

Sixth, let Jesus take care of the rest (vv. 12-16). Jesus's tone seems to change at this point. Scholars often try to determine whether these verses already reflect Jesus's own rejection of the towns (Mark 6:1-6) or whether Luke inserted this language because the towns opposed the Jesus movement following the resurrection. The stark imagery includes previous disobedient cities such as Sodom (of Sodom and Gomorrah infamy in Gen. 18–19). The practice of sackcloth and ashes in the Phoenician cities of Tyre and Sidon reminds readers of the land of Nineveh, once visited by Jonah, the reluctant prophet (Jon. 3:6-9). Now before we adopt a smug view that Jesus will "take care of" unbelievers, we need to realize that the cities under condemnation—Chorazin (Matt. 11:20-24), Bethsaida (Mark 8:22-26), and even Capernaum, Jesus's home (Matt. 4:13)—all represent cities on the northern shore of the Sea of Galilee, where Jesus himself visited. In a nutshell, these cities receive condemnation for their rejection of Jesus and God the Father based on their familiarity with the gospel, not the disciples' recent witness.

Luke 10:17-23 records the successful return of the seventy-two. The response seems rather dramatic by any imagination: demons submitting, Satan falling, snakes and scorpions crushed underfoot. If we feel as if we are in an action-hero movie, so do our journalists-turned-scholars. The language, while overly dramatic ("apocalyptic" might be the best term), really represents the promise and the power of the disciples' gospel message, by the power of the Holy Spirit (v. 21). Jesus seems to be signaling that fulfilling the missional call of the disciples can provide dramatic results. When fulfilled, the disciples get a glimpse of the fullness of the kingdom of God often missed by many passionate and powerful people before them.

The Good Samaritans

Some people might end this study on such a high note, observing that any disciple, when she or he fulfills her or his missional calling, can create dramatic results. However, lest confidence changes to arrogance, Luke provides one more story by Jesus to offer a sobering reminder as we close this study. Even in the middle of this declaration of success, Luke introduces a nosy lawyer who seeks to balance this seemingly cosmic promise of the kingdom of God with his personal need for eternal life. Jesus seems to treat this person as a kind of know-it-all who quickly gets to the textbook answer of loving God and loving neighbor (Luke 10:25-28). Then the lawyer, just to justify himself, decides to push the point by asking, "And who is my neighbor?" (v. 29). Jesus tells the story of the good Samaritan.

A traveler is assaulted along the road to Jericho and left for dead on the side of the road. Two religious Jewish leaders pass by and intentionally ignore the hurt man (probably for religious reasons). But then a Samaritan appears. Moved to compassion, the Samaritan cares for the man, takes him to an inn for recovery, and pays for his expenses. Jesus fires back to the lawyer: "'Which of these three do you think was a neighbor to the man who fell into the hands of robbers?' The expert in the law replied, 'The one who had mercy on him.' Jesus told him, 'Go and do likewise'" (vv. 36-37, NIV).

In other words, rather than worrying *who* is our neighbor, we should decide to *be* a neighbor to others. Truthfully, the story proves interesting in and of itself, but why does Luke include it on the heels of one of the biggest missionary efforts seen in the Gospels?

Samaritans possess a muddy history when it comes to their relationship with the Jewish people. Seen as ethnic half-breeds, their story goes back to Nehemiah. However, current Samaritan villages probably emerged during the time between the Old and New Testaments. The Samaritan people adhere to a closed-minded vision of the Jewish religion, following only the first five books of the Bible (known as the Torah) and worshipping on Mount Gerizim.[4] The presence of a caring Samaritan probably shocked the young lawyer and the other Jews listening, as a surprising addition.

For those reading along in Luke, Jesus's selection of a Samaritan in this parable (a metaphorical story with a "bite" inside it) may also seem a surprise. Just prior to the sending of the seventy-two disciples, Jesus encounters a Samaritan village that rebuffs Jesus's presence and prompts the "fiery" response of James and John in Luke 9:51-56, which we recounted in chapter 2.

However, Jesus may also have in mind a different encounter with another "good Samaritan." The meeting occurred with a Samaritan woman at a well where the Savior rested (John 4:1-42), following an intense period during which Jesus's disciples baptized a number of new converts (vv. 2-4).

---

4. James D. Purvis, "Samaritans," in *HarperCollins Bible Dictionary*, 964-66; H. G. M. Williamson, "Samaritans," in *New Bible Dictionary*, 1062-63.

While the disciples depart for food, Jesus uses a simple request for a drink of water to introduce this woman to "living water" through faith in Christ (v. 10). Much like Mary Magdalene, the family story often portrays our heroine as a shamed woman, with multiple marriages, rather than a dispirited religious leader. Some journalist-scholars offer that the five "husbands," or lords, in John 4:18 could represent either the five pagan gods that the original Samaritans in the Bible worshipped (2 Kings 17:30-31) or the five books of the Torah that occupy the center of current Samaritan devotion.[5]

From Jesus's perspective, the missional call lies not just with the seventy-two but also with the compassion and witness of those least likely to be considered disciples, much less evangelists.

---

5. Holmes and Lyons, *John 1–12*, 131-32.

The conversation then moves to worship on Mount Gerizim, the other central act of Samaritan religious devotion, and ultimately to the disclosure by Jesus that he is the Messiah (John 4:21-26). The woman's response includes her return to her village. Based on her testimony, and the same invitation to "come and see" that Andrew used with Nathanael (v. 29; 1:46), a number of Samaritans come running to see Jesus and invite him to their village, where he would ultimately stay another two days (4:27-42).

The Twelve, returning from seeking hospitality and food, worry about Jesus's well-being. Seeing the Samaritans running to him, Jesus offers the observation that fulfilling this gospel mission is food enough for him and offers an observation about harvests and laborers (vv. 34-38), reminiscent of his commission in Luke 10. From Jesus's perspective, the missional call lies not just with the seventy-two but also with the compassion and witness of those least likely to be considered disciples, much less evangelists, in Jesus's day.

Joining the Journey

One thing remains clear from the stories of the sending of the Twelve and the seventy-two: disciples have a mission. Many readers often start with the apostles in Acts 2 to talk about the mission of the church. Or often they circle back to Jesus's Great Commission following his resurrection in Matthew 28:16-20. Yet discipleship under Jesus begins much earlier, when twelve fledgling disciples and at least seventy-two other followers in training found themselves on the job "learning by doing" through proclaiming the good news of the kingdom of God. Yes, Jesus provided clear commands for them; yes, real ministry happened; and yes, Jesus saw the power of God at work in and through these newly minted disciples.

Our lives as disciples should prove no different. Jesus's commission then to the disciples remains our commission now. Missional outreach remains necessary work for all disciples as we journey together to speak peace, make a difference in people's lives, provide a clear witness to the kingdom of God, deal with rejection, and let Jesus take care of the rest. The six rules that guided the mission of the seventy-two can also guide our mission today. Recognizing that there are no lone-ranger missionaries might go a long way toward recovering collaboration as an essential part of outreach. Balancing the privilege of Jesus's call with real-life challenges might help us set more realistic outcomes for others and for ourselves. Learning to speak peace and offer respect first, even before mentioning repentance, may remind us of the real goal of the kingdom of God. Seeking the well-being of others but keeping the kingdom of God in full view balances our priorities. Learning how to deal with rejection and recognizing that often the greatest offenders are people who have the closest relationship with Jesus's message may help us recognize where accountability really lies and ultimately who provides the final judgment. These principles provide reasonable rules for any disciple ready to pick up Jesus's mission on earth.

However, the stories of these two "good Samaritans" also carry several messages at this juncture of the journey. The first message in the parable of the good Samaritan may challenge any thinking that fulfilling our missional call justifies our own place as disciples. People who try to justify themselves often get what they deserve based on their own human frailty. But the bigger message involves the exemplars in these stories. An unnamed Samaritan man provides the first model of a truly compassionate disciple, someone willing to show compassion when the religious "blinders" of the so-called people of God (the Jewish leaders) prevent them from seeing the real need.

The Samaritan woman demonstrates both personal attention and missional passion by calling people to meet Jesus, even when the twelve disciples appear more interested in their well-being than in meeting their job description. When we accept our missional mandate, and even when that mandate goes well, we still need to maintain a dose of humility to avoid thinking the kingdom of God is our private possession. Often Jesus, through the Holy Spirit, may well be at work in people we least expect. We need to accept our role as disciples, but we do not get to define who else might be a disciple. Discipleship remains both a gift and a mandate in which God always works through people, places, and communities that we might least expect. Alongside commitment and courage, we disciples need to show compassion, hospitality, and even humility as hallmarks of true discipleship.

Discussion Questions

1. When people hear the word "mission" or "missions" in the church, what normally comes to their minds?

2. Can disciples, early in their journey, serve as good witnesses of the kingdom of God? Why or why not?

3. Can missional engagement actually serve as a way of discipling Christians? How?

4. Why would Jesus lift up people that most of the disciples might normally ignore, perhaps even despise, as examples of compassion and outreach?

5. Are there "Samaritans" in our communities that might be doing the work of the kingdom of God that we overlook? How can we learn from them?

Scripture Studies: Missionary Comparisons

- Comparing the Missional Call of the Twelve and the Seventy-Two: Mark 6:7-13; Luke 9:1-6; 10:1-16
- Comparing the Good Samaritans' Behavior: Luke 10:25-37; John 4:1-26
- Comparing the Response of the Seventy-Two and the Response of the Samaritan Leader: Luke 10:17-24; John 4:27-42

EPILOGUE

❖ As you journeyed through these eight chapters, I hope you found a group of people not that much different from people of today. As disciples, we may well find ourselves behaving in one or more of the following ways:

- Moving to action before reflection
- Seeking social status or at least feeling a kind of social "insecurity" born from a lack of love
- Seeing the world through skeptical lenses or mired in the mild hopelessness of the times
- Feeling different from the normal crowd due to culture or a questionable personal past
- Wondering just what we might have to offer, since we seem to have so little to give
- Wrestling with a violent past or being tempted to take things into our own hands
- Seeking to be empowered as women in a male-dominated world
- Finding our calling but struggling to remain both compassionate and hospitable to people unlike ourselves

Any of these all-too-human feelings and behaviors not only influence our discipleship but also shape our lives.

However, one thing remains consistent no matter who we are. The constant promise for all disciples is the loving presence of Jesus Christ, the full representation of the grace of God the Father, living in the world today through the ongoing presence of the Holy Spirit. Regardless of our individuality, we live our lives together as disciples in the body of Christ, the church. As we join this relational journey as disciples, we should remember just how much we are bound together, not just by our common need but also by the overflow of the grace of God. This grace, through the Holy Spirit, transforms our natural relationships into a bond of covenant love for one another and for Jesus.

My prayer, much like Paul's prayer for the Ephesians (3:14-21), is that you not only will know the height and depth of God's love in and through Jesus Christ but also will open yourselves up to the Holy Spirit so that together you will fully manifest this love both for God and for your neighbors as you live out the missional life of discipleship.